YOU'RE DOING GREAT SWEETIE

A Guide to Inner Transformation

Kirsty Stewart

You're Doing Great Sweetie

You're Doing Great Sweetie

Copyright © 2020 Kirsty Stewart

The moral right of the author to be identified as the author of this work has been asserted.

The author of this book intends for its content to be referred to for general use in the quest for wellbeing. It does not dispense professional medical advice or prescribe treatment of any kind. The information intends to be used in conjunction with a responsible program prescribed by a health care professional. In the event you choose to employ the contents of this book the author assumes no responsibility for your actions and is in no way liable for any misuse of material.

Find more information at: kirstystewart.net.au

Connect with the author on Instagram @iam_kirsty

Cover design copyright © 2020 Katy Hulton

DEDICATION

This book is dedicated to us;
because we deserve it.

CONTENTS

Acknowledgments

Thank you to my parents for your unwavering love and support. Your continual encouragement has given me permission to believe in myself. Thank you to my sister Lisa, and to my brother Shane for generously lending me your time and expertise, you inspire me in ways you could never know. Thank you to Milly for your enduring advice and support. I have gratefully soaked up every word of wisdom you have imparted to me. Thank you to Katy for your generous help with the cover design. And finally, thank you to all my close friends who cheer my every success.

PART ONE

Transformation Of The Inner World

'Give up defining yourself - to yourself or to others. You won't die. You will come to life. And don't be concerned with how others define you. When they define you, they are limiting themselves, so it's their problem. Whenever you interact with people, don't be there primarily as a function or a role, but as the field of conscious Presence. You can only lose something that you have, but you cannot lose something that you are.'

-Eckhart Tolle

1.1 The cardinal rules of nature

'When we are no longer able to change the situation, we are challenged to change ourselves.'

- Viktor Frankl

Life is focused on only one thing: the here and now. Our source of power comes from connecting to the infinite potential of the present moment by disintegrating illusions that insist on alienation from wellbeing. When our attention is focused on the here and now we activate freedom to choose any emotion or thought from infinite potential. This kind of focus provides the opportunity to create an entirely new reality by choosing new thoughts in support of a new vision. A potential reality emerges on the physical plane when we consistently think new thoughts that provoke new habits of action. A common ailment in thinking that causes great inner turmoil and distress is that the outside world exists independently of the inner world. Many people are unaware that to initiate change in their circumstances they must first shift the world that harbors within. It is entirely possible to create the life of our dreams by undergoing the journey of inner transformation that ensues a shift in awareness from the illusion of separation to the truth of oneness.

Dr. Joe Dispenza writes in his book, *Breaking the Habit of Being Yourself,* that this is not a Newtonian world of cause and effect as we once thought; we are in actuality causing an effect with our thoughts and emotions. We are not linear beings living in a linear universe governed by time. We live in a world of duality that allows us to exist in a paradox. We may think we are separate from the chair we are sitting on but this is an illusion that allows us to explore endless potential realities. This illusion serves us by reflecting back to us what we think about but can prove harmful if we identify with what we see.

Unfortunately many people believe they are victims to circumstance as they have forgotten they are so powerful they can create a reality that reflects powerlessness. Those who are amorphous with their intentions in life experience this as a vague feeling of dissatisfaction whereas those who are deliberate with their thinking experience more joy. Interestingly, the ones who struggle believe their advice to be more pertinent than those in connection with their wellbeing. That is because love requires nothing and seeks to change no one as it sees everything as perfect. Everyone has their own inner being calling them home and it is our choice whether we respond to the invitation for greatness.

Inner transformation closes the gap between where we are and where we want to be by inviting us to reassess the beliefs that shape our reality. Change becomes possible when we understand that what we perceive of as reality is a sensory interpretation of thought and that the ideal future we imagine to be so distant is actually at our fingertips. What we seek to acquire in a desired experience is a feeling of joy, which can be experienced in the present moment. The process of creation instigates an evolution in thinking as we identify what we do not want, paint a new vision of what we do want and think new thoughts in support of the vision. The quickest way to do this is by contemplating what thoughts we would think if we were already living our desired reality. What prevents most people from creating their ideal reality is identification with existing circumstances and attachment to fear. Most of us are taught at a young age that what we see is who we are. Our elders teach, 'this is who we are and this what our people do.' As we grow to identify with the thinking patterns of our elders we cease evolution and maintain a standard reality that becomes the platform for potential. In order to break this pattern we must be bold enough to break identification with the tribe and think differently. Mediocrity is achieved with mediocre thoughts; greatness is achieved with great thoughts. What we currently see evidence of amongst younger generations who face the burden of a collapsing world is a push against traditional thought patterns that produce suffering. More people are being pulled by the universal vision for love and peace we are in dire need of.

Those who live in fear expect others to change whereas the empowered ones change their inner world regardless of what is going on around them. The fear mind is a personification of the illusion of separation that underlies much of what we encounter. It is trapped in the insane idea that a higher power has condemned us to a life of suffering as retribution for our sins and that we must earn forgiveness to earn the right to die peacefully. In other words, we live in hell to die in peace. This misconception of abandonment implies we must employ ourselves for the role of God. What impossible shoes to fill! Rather than living life joyously as a channel for divine inspiration we spend our time trying to prove our worth with the acquisition of wealth. The fear mind is a collection of thoughts and opinions based on past experiences that do not allow new ways of thinking that threaten its identity as ruler. It requires stability instead of freedom, permanence in place of change, vigilance over trust and stagnation of evolution. This way of thinking causes chronic illness and extreme negative emotional states such as bipolar, depression and anxiety. This type of fear surpasses the primal extinct for survival and permeates into a state of being that becomes our experience of reality.

The key to transforming fear into love is to understand that nothing is ever permanent. We simply choose to think the same thoughts that produce repeated experience but when our attention is on the present moment we have access to infinite potential of thought. The only way we can appear to be separate from that which we are is with the existence of duality. But in order to invite change we must eradicate the idea we are separate from the stream of wellbeing and understand that we are physical beings living out the manifestation of the non-physical. It is impossible for us to experience anything other than that which is a match to our thoughts. Our love of story telling is a gift we can use to create the life of our dreams but can also trap us into thinking we are what we experience. Studies have shown that an emotion typically passes through awareness between six to ninety seconds but it is the story we tell about the emotion that escalates it into a belief. These stories create the illusion of continuity and justify why we are the way we are. Fear takes the emotion personally and judges the experience so that it evolves into a trauma whereas unconditional love allows the experience to pass through awareness without forming conclusions. This is a skill that can easily be honed with consistent questioning of what is true.

Fear is jealous and assigns blame. It expects others to be consistent in the behaviour they offer to prevent its identity being threatened and experiences extreme upset when others express change. For example, a woman who is cheated on by her partner may conclude all men are pigs as a way of making sense of the pain. To prevent the outcome from reoccurring the disempowered person enacts revenge and seeks approval from the outside world. The empowered person uses the experience as an opportunity to look at what beliefs caused the experience without assigning blame by evolving into a state of being that allows more love. Many times the chronic negative experiences we encounter are manifestations of unprocessed childhood traumas. The negative emotion drawn from the experience becomes a state of being from which life creates from and reacts to. If we ask for a new experience and do not transform the inner world, the desired manifestation will only come through a filter of suffering.

Transformation of the inner world arrives when the desire for greatness outweighs the habit of remaining limited. A crisis calls into question all we think we know and prompts us to choose growth or stagnation. If we choose to remain the same it is likely we will experience another crisis until we choose evolution. That is not because we are at the mercy of the universe, but because we *are* the universe asking ourselves to accept the call to greatness. That is the great paradox, we are the universe experiencing itself in physical form through the illusion of separation. Once we are aware we are living in this paradox we can begin to deliberately create the life of our dreams. If we are going to think at all, why not think big? Why not think loving thoughts that bring about joy, peace and abundance? When our intention to experience greatness transcends the excuses of the fear mind such as, 'this doesn't feel right,' or, 'this is spiritual hog wash,' we can see with clarity the lies we have previously adhered to. This is not a 'how to' book that provides strategies for fixing what is damaged. This book has been created to guide you home to the truth that dwells within. This book is here to remind you that you are doing great, that in the eyes of source it is impossible for anything to wrong, and it is simply what you choose to experience. If you do not like it choose again, and if you do, keep it up. When we choose to believe life supports us we will see every experience as an opportunity to grow.

1.2 Processing trapped emotions

'The artist is no other than he who unlearns what he has learned, in order to know himself.'

- E.E. Cummings

Blocked energy in the body is simply unexpressed emotion. When a child is upset they express their emotion in the moment of occurrence and move on satisfied they have spoken their truth. An adult's reaction tends to go deeper and can sometimes last a lifetime. Resentments form, things are taken personally, stories are invented to justify pain, vengeance is proclaimed in the face of injustice, love is shared sparingly and hearts are closed in fear of punishment. Imagine a child whose toy was stolen by a classmate; do they say, 'I'll see you in court' and declare that it will never play with another toy again to eliminate the chance of having something stolen from them? What is more likely is that they will throw a tantrum, perhaps shed a fear tears and snatch it back, but at the end of the day the incident will have been forgotten.

As we grow older we place importance on self-image, how others perceive us, and how we fit in the world. We craft a persona that feels comfortable in a world where it does not feel safe to express our authentic selves. If this false sense of identity is created from unprocessed emotions such as betrayal we create betrayal-generating experiences. We may create an identity for many reasons including safety, ignorance or attention, which then shows up in experiences that generate the same emotional reactions usually because it supports an identity of victimhood. Susan Kerr explains in her book *The System for Soul Memory*, that all emotions stored in the body are a result of events that occur before the age of eight and that every event after that is a reincarnation of memory. Therapists commonly explore a patient's childhood to identify the sponsoring trauma and psychologists often regress at least three generations.

To begin the process of healing let us use the situation that caused distress to fully feel into the emotion. Contemplate how it made us feel and allow the story behind it to unfold without attachment. The point of feeling a trapped emotion is not to believe the story but to hear it, love it and have compassion for its pain. Our mind will likely throw up an endless array of excuses to stop us from accessing the core emotion in fear that its argument will be exposed with thoughts like:

- I thought I was done with this
- This is too painful to feel
- This is all his fault
- They are the reason I'm in pain
- I hate them
- I don't want to feel weak
- Winners don't cry
- If I feel this emotion they will win
- This wouldn't have happened if I were…
- I can deal with this later
- There's no point
- There's no coming back from this pain

Resist the urge to berate yourself and rest in the knowledge that only the small self can be upset. The greater you, your inner being, the light at the center can never feel anything other than love. The deeper we dig into ourselves the more love we will find because that is what we are made up of. If we use our mind to understand the nature of our being we will never find what we are looking for but when we feel our way there we achieve clarity. Becoming aware of trapped emotions is important to understanding that the story behind them is illusory, they are just visitors. They are indicators that the thoughts we are thinking are not a match with what life thinks about us. Emotions arise in the mind like waves crossing an ocean. We are the infinite ocean and life passes through us in little ripples that might disrupt the surface but at the heart we are unchanged and unmoved. Nothing in this world is permanent and trying to make it so only causes suffering. When a strong emotion arises the fear mind will have developed a very clever way of automatically deflecting it to avoid feeling the pain. Avoiding feeling the emotion perpetuates the story that supports suffering and limits our capacity to feel joy. To completely transform and transcend the emotion we must, if we can, catch it in the moment. Once we are fully present in the moment we can ask these questions:

1. What emotion am I feeling?
2. Where do I feel this emotion in my body?
3. If this emotion could tell me anything, what would it say?
4. What would it take for me to release it?
5. How would I feel if it was released?

These kinds of open-ended questions cause us to search for answers and past experiences where we once felt liberated. Being inquisitive with our emotions immediately weakens their power and opens us up to the possibility of awakening. Shining light unto the dark reveals the holes in the beliefs that keep us small and allows us to begin thinking new thoughts that support a life of love. Consistently asking if we are really upset for the reason we think will open doorways to new ways of beings that radically transform our life for the better.

1.3 Asking empowering questions

'Every next level of your life will demand a different you.'

- Paulo Coelho

Contemplation is an essential part of healing that allows our mind to lightly ponder the vastness of the universe and the role we want to play in it. It does not involve critical analysis of the past or what we could have done differently but rather awareness on what is present within us. We weaken the bonds of our past by focusing on the power of the present moment and using that as our foundation for imagining a life of greatness. There is no way we can feel the most joy we have ever experienced if we are using the past as a baseline for our new imaginings. Inner transformation is a journey just like any other that begins with a conscious decision to change and the willingness to follow through. Asking empowering questions invites curiosity that causes us to contemplate whether our current beliefs serve us and what we can replace them with.

Disempowering questions reinforce victimhood and prevent us from reaching our full potential such as, 'why me? How could this happen to me? How could they do this to me? What did I do to deserve this? What did I do wrong? How can I fix this? Why am I broken?' These types of questions cause the fear mind to provide us with memories of past experiences that support suffering. We will never receive an honest answer to these questions because they do not exist; we are not victims. If we want to receive honest answers we must ask ourselves questions that imply the universe exists to benefit us. We are alchemists; we can turn negative energy into positive energy by focusing our awareness on what is beneficial. Types of questions we want to consistently ask that prompt the universe to prove its support include:

- What is the purpose of my life?
- What is my life calling?
- How can this situation be here for my benefit?
- What if this situation is actually propelling me to my life calling?
- What is trying to emerge in my life?
- What gift do I have to give?
- How can I be of service?
- How much power can flow through me?
- What idea does the universe want to express through me?
- How am I making my life more difficult than it needs to be?
- What do I need to let go of to manifest my vision?
- What habits and thought patterns must change?
- What does it feel like to live my vision?
- What if the universe is conspiring for my good?
- How can it get better than this?
- What kind of emotions do I want to feel in my envisioned life?
- What difference do I want to make?

When we feel ourselves having a conditioned negative emotional response to something, our habitual response is it to judge it but if we can remain in our center as it passes it will not become part of our story. A negative habit can only be changed once we satisfy the need it is fulfilling internally, which eliminates addictions, codependency and neediness. Change occurs incrementally the more we are willing to look at the illusions that restrict us from living a life of greatness. With consistent awareness of the truth and willingness to release attachment to suffering what remains will be both nothingness and everything for this is a return to oneness. Fighting, judging or condemning an emotion is a tool of the fear mind that holds us apart from achieving success. Many people are willing to admit their life could be much worse but few are willing to admit it could be much better.

What is your vision? What do you want to transform into? What are you giving birth to? The struggle a caterpillar encounters to break free of its cocoon develops strength in its muscles that equip it for the outside world. Inner transformation is akin to the transformation of a caterpillar as we retreat into the cocoon of the self; find inner strength and then show up as our true authentic self. Outgrowing old skin can at times feel painful but all we are releasing is the pain of attachment and once we clear out stagnant beliefs we will blossom into the true self. We will no longer feel the urge to replace our identity with a new false sense of self and instead will see the value in the formless, unidentifiable spirit that is us.

1.4 Our inner being

'If you want something you've never had, you have to do something you've never done.'

- Thomas Jefferson

Beyond the voice of safety, the voice of desire and the voice of knowledge there is an eternal, ever present being that remains unchanged and full of love, which we will refer to as our inner being. It alludes to the part of us that is always in connection with the divine and in communion with universal knowledge. It is the ocean dwelling within always rooted in the truth, beckoning us to its stream of wellbeing that provides all ideas. Our inner being observes all life experience without judgment including our reactions for it resides in the awareness of love, which we have access to at all times. Our goal is not to make ourselves worthy of access to this stream through prayer, retribution or forgiveness; it is to relinquish the illusion that we are separate. It is impossible to be separate from that which we are, therefore waste no time entertaining the insane idea that we are alone and must suffer to have our needs met. If we learn how to treat life like it is our best friend we will see evidence of its support everywhere, even in circumstances we may think of as negative.

If we defend our story with guilt, shame or anger we slow the stream of wellbeing that inevitably flows to and through us so that our vision is distorted. When this occurs we interpret experiences that ask us to change as punishment and experiences that bring joy as conditional. When we believe in the fallacy of separateness we forget who we are but our inner being is always calling us to awaken. In an episode of the kid's television program *Avatar: The Last Airbender*, the character of an Indian guru describes the process of clearing the chakras to unblock access to the stream of wellbeing. Each chakra is its own pool of energy and when one gets blocked it inhibits the flow to all other pools. The guru says sometimes life can get muddy and we have to clear the gunk that dirties these pools. The gunk he refers to is the limiting beliefs we accumulate from childhood, the emotions we hold onto, the grudges we enforce and so on. Pride is a tool of the fear mind that grasps limiting beliefs but when we step into awareness we see these limitations and lovingly release them back into the nothingness from which they came. Learning how to clear these pools is an ongoing process that requires awareness, compassion and consistency.

Mind attacks are temporary relapses in awareness that cause us to have extreme emotional attachment to our identity. These attacks can allude us into thinking that the effort we have put into changing has been made redundant, but it is simply the energy clearing the path for more good to come. There are no step backs on the journey to inner transformation because our vision for a better life is more powerful than the fear mind's desire to remain small. Despite what our circumstances may appear to be life has conspired through the path of least resistance a way to deliver to us everything we have asked for. Attempting to configure *how* we will get there is futile and impossible for our minds to discover, as it will happen in a way we cannot predict. Instead we must remind ourselves *why* we want it so we know what to look for. When we feel a mind attack pulling us back into the story behind the negative emotion it takes less effort to feel the emotion than it does to resist it, because eventually with consistent awareness they will disappear. Express how you feel in the moment even if it hurts with words like, 'they betrayed me,' 'I feel abandoned,' 'if I'd known better none of this would have happened,' 'I loathe myself.' These are the thoughts you have been secretly harbouring but never allowed yourself to admit. It takes courage to express an emotion and admit the truth about how you feel.

An important step to transforming our inner world is to completely accept where we are. When a mind attack strikes and we fall back into the momentum of negative energy the easiest way out it is to go with it. In the film *Harry Potter and the Philosopher's Stone* the three main characters pass through an entanglement of live vines to get closer to the philosopher's stone. With trepidation they try to slide through using force only to realise if they fought through the vines it would strangle them so the way to pass through was by relaxing and holding still. The same is true of a mind attack; our initial response is to resist and fight against the entanglement of negative emotion but the more we fight back the stronger it holds us. To escape we need to relax and allow the wave to wash over our ocean.

When we consciously choose to live a life of greatness we must be willing to contemplate the presence of limiting thoughts and beliefs and allow the energy of change to move through our body. It is almost like we have to give up our power to gain power. A clear intention initiates momentum in the direction of where we want to go but we must temporarily ride out the momentum of where we have been going before we begin to see physical evidence of change. The first sign of evidence we will notice is a feeling of lightness, joy and gratitude which may then be quickly countered by strong feelings of guilt, shame and betrayal. This may feel disheartening but it is the fear mind's natural response to change and is a sign we are on the right track. During this time what may appear as regression is actually progression in disguise for there is no such thing as a step backwards. Intense mind attacks are the energy's way of stirring up that which no longer serves us so that we can be free of the insane story of separation that causes suffering. If we are clear with our intentions life will conspire to make our dreams a reality.

Knowing how to process a mind attack is an empowering tool we can use throughout our lives when we encounter difficult people or circumstances. Life is supposed to be fun but not everyday is sunny and we must prepare for the storms that come our way so that we do not dive into despair. When we clear the flow of our inner being we understand how to manage the highs and lows of life without becoming attached to an outcome. Bipolar is a symptom of attachment to the fear mind that causes emotional instability. Once we fully understand that we are supported and adored by life our reactions to circumstances become less extreme and we allow emotions to pass through with ease. The fear mind thrives off attention and will throw a tantrum in the most cunning of ways so that we feel we have no control but when we become stubborn with what we give our attention to we discover power in the face of conditions that make us feel powerless. This power will not be acquired over night but will become stronger very quickly when consistency meets momentum.

1.5 Transforming breakdowns into breakthroughs

'Don't let your happiness depend on something you may lose.'

-C.S. Lewis

Breakdowns occur when an over accumulation of resistance is released from the body through an emotional channel. Using the story of the chakras, it is when too much gunk blocks the stream flowing between each pool of energy and the force of negative emotion accumulates until eventually it breaks free. What may feel severely unpleasant at the time is actually the body's natural response to blocked energy and lifts us from a feeling of powerlessness to a more energised state of hope. It is important during our time of transformation to not wish to jump from powerlessness to exponential happiness too quickly as it may dissuade us from achieving our goal.

When we stand at the bottom of a mountain we do not plan every path we will take or every rock we will tread, we simply take the first step and gradually work our way up knowing that each step will reveal itself one at a time. If we stand in the position of powerlessness the road to happiness can be daunting and may make us want to cower in fear but if we take each step on the emotional scale as it comes we have a better chance of surviving the journey. Too often people overestimate what they can achieve in a year and underestimate what they can achieve in five years. Forcing ourselves to feel happy despite the intensity of negative emotion that bubbles within is counterintuitive and will slow down our path to healing but if we relax, remain open and keep breathing the universe will deliver to us the perfect path to our desires.

If we set our goals too high or place an unrealistic time frame on them the disparity between where we are and where we want to go will not motivate us to continue. There is no need for us to know everything right away. A helpful question we can ask during a mind attack is, 'will achieving what I want right this instant truly make me feel better?' You might say, 'well I'd rather be crying in a hot tub than in this run down car,' but sadness is sadness no matter where it is felt. Achieving the perfect outer world will not fill a void; it is a byproduct of achieving inner harmony. The sooner we cease placing our source of happiness on material success the sooner we can allow in more joy. The pathway is not a straight line and sometimes we jump too high then fall back but no matter what direction we are going we are always on the right path. The linear emotional journey to peace looks like this:

Powerlessness => apathy => despair => sadness => blame => anger => hope => excitement => anticipation =>expectation => contentment => joy => peace.

What will inhibit and slow down our journey to peace is attachment to the stories that support the idea of the small self. Each time we mentally relive the event that caused us pain we activate the neurons in the brain that cause us to think the same thoughts of betrayal, powerlessness, sadness or other negative emotion connected to the event. We tell the story again and again, analyse it, blame, wish it did not happen, pray for justice, plan vengeance, wonder how it could have ended differently, question what went wrong, say 'if only', and the list goes on. When this occurs the resistance to our inner being becomes so strong that a breakdown becomes our savior.

Non-attachment is a process that relies on the fluidity of awareness. Despite the pain, breakdowns can be a wonderful way of loosening attachments and clarifying our vision, though they should not be made into a habit due to their detrimental nature. Their purpose is to liberate us from emotional stagnation and give us the freedom to change. Once the breakdown has passed and the dust settled intend on modifying behaviours that allow negative emotions to pass through without judgment or condemnation. Not everything in life has to be perfect for us to start feeling happy right now. Empowering questions we can use to begin weakening the charge behind negative emotions triggered by a memory include:

- How can I use this situation to empower me?
- Does rejection truly make me less worthy?
- Does it really matter if this person wanted to hurt me?
- Is this situation truly inhibiting my ability to manifest my desires?
- Does anything anyone says or does have anything to do with me?

When we operate under the assumption that we are absolutely adored by life and always in connection with our inner being the actions of another will not affect us. If someone attempts to pull us down to their level by hurting, scolding or rejecting us we will say, 'so what? I know who I am, I know I am worthy of love and whether you show me love or not I will always show up for me.' Some will find this infuriating as they try to fish a reaction from us. No matter our relation to another or how long we have known them we do not need attention or approval from anyone apart from ourselves and the sooner we understand this the quicker the gap closes. We become overflowing with love when we consistently direct our awareness on the ever-abundant stream of wellbeing that flows to us at all times. When this occurs we are fed by life itself and not the empty external reality that is but a mere reflection of our thoughts. Promise yourself that you will always show up for you no matter the circumstance.

Author Brené Brown says in her book *Daring Greatly*, 'vulnerability is not winning or losing; it's having the courage to show up and be seen when we have no control over the outcome. Vulnerability is not weakness; it's our greatest measure of courage.' Have the courage to show up as your true authentic self and speak your truth. We will have reached liberation when we can say 'so what? I still love myself,' even in the face of rejection. Soon enough our unconditional self love will be so strong and unshakeable that we will feel no emotional charge when someone tries to belittle us. When this happens our standards rise, we find comfort in solitude, and we will encounter people who feel compelled to reflect back to us our state of love so that it becomes our predominant experience. We will have broken through the story of the fear mind and have compassion for those still finding their way.

1.6 Employing positive self-talk

'Trade your expectation for appreciation and the whole world changes for you.'

- Anthony Robbins

Becoming aware of our self-talk is a skill that requires consistency, patience and non-judgment. It is said we think around 60 000 thoughts a day; that is a lot of opportunity for us to direct our thoughts in the direction of our dreams. Becoming aware of every single thought will drive us insane but we can get an idea of what we predominately think about by paying attention to the way we feel and how we communicate with others. When we think about something long enough it activates a vibration that becomes a mood and if the mood is sustained for a long period of time it becomes a temperament, and if that temperament is sustained for longer than three months it becomes a personality trait.

For example, if you are driving to work and someone cuts you off in traffic the incident may aggravate you, but you have a choice in how long you react. If you allow the experience to pass through your awareness you will experience a brief feeling of annoyance but will soon forget the incident. If you judge the experience and identify with it the negative emotion escalates into a bad mood that affects the whole day. It may trigger the story of the small self and prompt you to ask disempowering questions like, 'why me? Why couldn't they just be patient? Why am I sitting in traffic to go to a job I hate when I could be at the beach? Why didn't I do a university degree in music and not accounting? If only I was smart enough, rich enough, more loved, had more supportive parents, or knew what my purpose was then I wouldn't be feeling this way.' This string of thoughts can be expressed either consciously or subconsciously in our mind. Often we are not even aware of the story we use as ammunition when triggered by adversity.

There is constant chatter going on in our minds reacting to what we see and finding ways we can identify with it. The mind says, 'what is my place? How do I fit into the world? How can I make this about me?' When a negative experience arises we question what we did to deserve it because fear believes we are at the mercy of life, but loves knows we are the creator. The stories and excuses of the fear mind are endless and judgmental. When we believe its stories they dominate our vibration and become a mood that attracts experiences generating like emotions. How do you talk to other people? What kind of phrases do you use? Do you say disempowering things like:

- That's the way the cookie crumbles
- God has his favourites
- That's just the way it is
- I could never afford something like that
- I want it but…
- It's just not in the cards for me
- I'd love to do _______ but that's for another lifetime
- I always seem to attract the ones with commitment issues
- Nobody takes me seriously
- I'm too old
- I'm too young
- I don't have enough experience
- I don't have the degree I need
- It will take too long to accomplish
- This always happens to me

When we become aware of the negative chatter that inhibits us from achieving our dreams we can begin the process of releasing our identity from the small self. To uncover every thought about each aspect of our lives would take much time and may take us further down the rabbit hole. To reveal our prevailing thoughts let us pay attention to the way we feel when the subject is activated. How do you feel when you talk about your finances? What do you say to people? Perhaps when you talk about money your shoulders slump and you hear yourself saying, 'I wish,' or, 'if only,' a lot. What is your mood when you talk about your career or your relationship with your partner? Pay attention to the way you feel and all answers will be revealed.

If we ask ourselves why we think a certain thought the mind will conjure various memories and opinions that support its argument but if we ask ourselves if the thought is true the mind will be exposed. You might have an idea for a creative project that would allow in more money, more fun and inspiring people but the mind counteracts the idea with a complaint about how long it would take to execute. In response you can say, 'is it really true that I don't have enough time? So what if it was true? It's only an opinion after all, and a very limited one too. In the time it takes to finish the creative project I will be doing the same thing I have always done so I might as well get started.' The mind may then complain about the possibility of failure to which we can ask, 'so what? People fail at doing things they hate so I might as well fail at doing something I love. The universe has my back no matter what happens.' This is a process that gently weakens our attachment to the mind without jumping too high.

1.7 Affirmations

'A real work of art destroys, in the consciousness of the receiver, the separation between himself and the artist.'

- Leo Tolstoy

Affirmations are a helpful tool for consciously introducing new and uplifting thoughts that support connection with our inner being. Empowering questions serve to weaken our attachment to limiting beliefs whereas affirmations give us the tools to create new beliefs in support of a new vision. When we are clear on what we wish to experience in our lives we are able to craft affirmations that help us get there. They are like statements to the universe about what we intend to experience before we live the full manifestation of them. They also help us to adjust to ways of thinking that produce action supporting an identity of success and love. Bill Gates does not think the same thoughts as the local gambling addict. What kind of thoughts would you think if you were already living your dream life? How would these thoughts feel? How would they inspire you to act? An empowered person does not think thoughts that match the vibration of victimhood; they deal with the emotion surrounding their circumstances and consciously make an effort to change their point of attraction using their thoughts. It is important to start general, then as we progress up the emotional scale we can begin to focus on specific things we want to change. An effective way of enforcing change is to write the affirmations on a piece of paper and read them throughout the day to be reminded of their message. It is like carrying around hope in physical form. Some good affirmations to start with are:

-	The universe is conspiring for my good
-	Life is on my side

- Everything is always working out for me
- I am connected to the stream of wellbeing
- I am beginning to see evidence of change
- I intend on living the life of my dreams
- I am willing to release all resistance
- I am open to changing and growing
- Life adores me and is always communicating with me

Consistently repeating affirmations throughout the day or at least a few times before bed slows the momentum of negative emotion and swings it in the direction of our dreams. It is important to understand that there is no need to believe these new thoughts at first. Gradually making them a part of our self-talk will help turn the tide so that these new potential thoughts evolve into a state of being. Inner transformation is impossible without believing that we are truly loved and supported by the universe. Older generations are more susceptible to believing life is a struggle as they have had more years to prove their story but they can change their story just as quickly as those who are younger. Once we are willing to release the idea that we are separate from our inner being we create space for new ways of being. With every moment comes a choice to think the same thoughts that create the same reality or think new thoughts that support a life of greatness.

We are liberated from suffering and operate with the knowingness that we are loved and supported when we are in alignment with our inner being. We will be attracted to people who uplift us and to opportunities that deliver abundance. Affirmations remind us of our vision and rewire our brain so that we focus awareness on what we want to experience. In time we will begin to love the process of creation and the timing of manifestation will become irrelevant. True liberation occurs when our happiness is based on how much love we are offering, not what is happening in the world around us. It is possible to change our thoughts about a specific subject without noticing the disparity between where we are and where we want to be. If repeating specific affirmations of wealth causes us to instead notice only lack then begin with general statements. Disempowering thoughts of wealth sound like:

- I never have enough
- I work pay cheque to pay cheque
- Any spare money I have I give away
- Money doesn't grow on trees
- Money is slow in coming
- The only way I can earn money is through the job I despise
- Just when I think I have enough another bill comes in the mail

When we shift our state of being from a point of lack to a general state of abundance we can tell a different story about money with affirmations like:

- I believe in the abundance of the universe
- There is plenty of money for everyone to be happy
- I have more money than I know what to do with
- Money comes to me in ways that are fun and easy
- I love my bills for they show me I can afford to pay them
- I am open to new ways of earning money

If we are too far down on the emotional scale and try to make ourselves feel better with affirmations about a specific subject we will be pulled down by the disparity between our dream and our current reality. But when we appreciate the universe for always guiding us, providing us with what we need, and for diligently responding to our questions we are in a better position to change a specific subject. Another prominent topic in our life we can construct affirmations for is relationships. Disempowering thoughts may sound like:

- I always attract the boys with commitment issues
- My wife never appreciates how hard I work
- My husband doesn't work hard enough
- They always leave me

- I'm scared they will hurt me so I hurt them first
- He never listens to me
- She doesn't stop nagging

Remember that people are only ever reflecting back to us our dominant vibration so when we have a trapped emotion of fear, rejection, loss, or betrayal we will become attracted to people who reflect them back to us. We will recreate situations that produce the same feeling of betrayal and abandonment as if we are living in *Ground Hog Day*, or in other words we will feel like we are living a repetition of the same scenario. This may show up in our experience of relationships as we hear the looming words, 'I'm just not ready to commit,' or they appear as emotionally unavailable. When we fill up our own cup with love and accept that it is our own responsibility to make ourselves happy we will begin to feel more love. The feeling of liberation emerges when we let everyone off the hook and say, 'I no longer need anyone to act or do anything to make me happy. I am showing up for myself and I intend on doing what I need to do to fill my own cup.' When we think loving thoughts about ourselves and about life we emanate a vibration of love, which is then radiated into the vibrational field and reflected back to us. This can show up as new people appearing in our life, troublesome people changing their attitude, or experiencing more affection from our loved ones. When we embody the feeling of love we create our experiences from this new point of attraction providing evidence of inner transformation. New thoughts we can say about relationships can be:

- I see evidence of love everywhere I go
- People reflect back to me the love I feel for myself
- I am in perfect harmony with those around me
- Love abounds me
- My relationships are fun and exciting
- My partner lovingly listens to what I say

The same applies for any aspect of our life. Whatever subject we want to focus on we can use affirmations as a tool for consciously changing our thoughts about it. While they are incredibly useful eventually we will go beyond them by integrating them into our self-talk. Positive self-talk elevates affirmations into a state of being so that creation becomes effortless. They are like a crutch we use to support our thoughts when we are run over by subconscious thinking patterns. If we feel only slight discomfort in our life we may only need them for a short time whereas if we are creating our life from the ground up we may find we need to use them a little longer. With consistent focus on the intention behind the affirmation they will soon become a way of life.

1.8 Making friends with change

'Allow yourself the uncomfortable luxury of changing your mind.'

It has been said the only thing constant in life is change. Why do we change? What is the point in evolution? Why not be born as the person we will end up being when we pass away? Why go through the trouble? From the perspective of the fear mind change can pose as a frivolous impedance to the structure of everyday life. When it seems like all we are here to do on this planet is work, pay the bills, feed the kids and have a few laughs in between, large-scale change can interrupt everything we know. But that is exactly the point of change; to challenge all we think we know. Author and spiritual leader Ram Dass says everything we see is born out of the formless and will one day return to its original state of nonexistence. The world was created out of nothing and we will once again return to that state at the point of death. In the emptiness we call 'Space' lays infinite potential for new thoughts, desires and manifestations. When we are born the potential of who we can be collapses in one moment of time but the possibility of who we can become is endless and constantly changing. We are under the illusion that we are separated from source at birth but in actuality we are born from it and therefore possess the same energy that holds infinite potential.

In a world of endless possibilities change allows us to focus on a potential reality and manifest it on the physical plane. Remaining fluid in our perception of what we think is concrete allows us to move with more flexibility between possible realities. If we remain rigid in what we think is real and what is possible for us we will only grow as much as we allow ourselves to but when we lose our mind we become the recipient to a world of infinite potential. When we are consumed by the fear mind and face large-scale change we are likely to reject life's call to expansion and fight to remain the same. Change is a contentious topic to the small-minded that will often encounter a rebuttal but if we exchange the energy we expend on resisting change with gratitude we will receive something of value. It takes less effort to think a pleasant thought than it does a negative thought so we might as well put our attention on something that adds value to our life.

In the realm of the non-physical change is instantaneous and requires no thought, whereas on the physical plane there is a delay in manifestation. What is the point in creating an incredibly dense reality that delays time between thought and manifestation when everything is instantly manifested in the non-physical? Well, because it is fun. The delay in manifestation gives us time to carefully curate what we wish to experience by allowing us to decipher what we want from what we do not want. The true delight is in watching the process of a desire unfold. People are inspired by stories of rags to riches where the protagonist experiences a radical inner transformation and decides to go for the life of their dreams rather than be held back by their circumstances.

When we watch movies or read books about change it is the suspense that makes it engaging. Can the person who experienced trauma use it to change their life for the better? Will the girl who was cheated on by her boyfriend love again? Will the father of a drug addict find a way to love his son? Contrasting experiences help our souls to evolve. Making friends with change allows us to find inner peace and remain in the heart of truth no matter our circumstances. Many people choose to remain unchanged and uninspired because it requires less effort to maintain existing beliefs and limitations than it does to think new thoughts. The decision to change is entirely personal preference and may decide to be acted upon or not depending on the intensity of desire for something greater. In some cases the decision to change may not be acted upon until a crisis occurs that initiates some form of 'soul searching,' which is our inner being's way of communicating to us the answer we are longing for cannot be found in the mind. For others it may come from a general sense of dissatisfaction or feeling like there is more to life than what they have been taught. The call to awakening is always beckoning us to its riches and is heard by those who refuse to accept things at face value.

The process of change can feel overwhelming especially for people who find sanctuary in remaining small. It is easier to feel like a victim, to perpetuate the momentum of suffering and concede the responsibility of owning our emotions rather than hold ourselves accountable for our own actions. It takes courage to deviate from what we have been taught and come face to face with the unknown but once we do we will become an inspiration to others and ourselves. Making the decision to change is a noble feat that gives us a reason to feel proud for choosing to venture into the unknown and live a life of greatness. For a small while there will be a period of uncertainty as we dispose of all we think we are and allow in new thoughts, beliefs and desires. Fragments of our old life will begin to fade away as we bring them to the light and contemplate who we wish to become but soon the potential of our dreams will become so strong that its essence outweighs the habit of remaining small. When we have the desire to experience something greater than ever before we inevitably expand our way of thinking to meet the reality of its potential. That is evolution.

Hastening the process of manifestation is counterproductive and serves no purpose other than to demonstrate we are not yet in alignment with its potential. In a world where success is primarily measured by wealth instead of happiness it is easy to feel like we have nothing to show for our time of transformation. This is when we may face temptation to revert back to old habits, reconnect with people who do not have our best interests at heart and find work that does not fulfill us in order to fill the void of emptiness. Know that emptiness is the space in which all potential resides. The fear mind will want to fill it with things of familiarity but when we make living our dreams a priority and refuse to accept anything less we will quickly pass through this phase of the journey. Patience allows us to achieve mental clarity and further refine new ideas. Feelings of lethargy and laziness are traditionally seen as negative emotions that hinder our journey to success but they are emotions we can benefit from. Terms like 'hustle' and 'daily grind' are commonly found in the vernacular of those who struggle to achieve their goals as it is yet another statement to the universe that we must struggle to have our needs met.

It feels like struggle when we place judgment on the feeling of laziness but if we can become comfortable with the temporary emptiness before the next idea arises we eliminate the risk of filling the void with detrimental habits. When we remove the contradictory thoughts that filter our connection to our stream of wellbeing we become the recipient to new and inspiring ideas. We also become intuitively aware of when is the right time to act and right time to rest. Life is a series of push and pull, in and out, up and down. Pushing through feelings of laziness robs us of the opportunity to allow new ideas and experiences to come to fruition. There is no drought in the world of the infinite. A metamorphosis is an intense and thorough process that transforms the entire inner world and can at times feel confronting. We must take care of the way we feel so if we are thinking thoughts like, 'I need this new project to work out so people don't think I'm a failure,' or, 'I have nothing to show for all the work I've done,' we are not being the beneficiary of our inner being. But if we change our thoughts to, 'I give myself permission to take my time,' and, 'I'm choosing to live a life of greatness to please me, no one else,' and, 'I release the need seek acceptance from anyone but myself,' we stay in the mood allowing for new ideas.

As we undergo the process of transformation we will encounter many of the fear mind's excuses to avoid the uncertainty change brings. It is as if the mind believes change is going to overthrow any last thread of dignity we may possess and that it would be better to continue critiquing our circumstances, blaming other people for the way we are and expecting things to remain the same. The fear mind says, 'why go to all this work when we can stay home, watch television and forget about everything? I have fun complaining with my friends about how the world is against me, how much my husband sucks and how much money we do not have. If I changed that would mean I would have to think different thoughts, do something different, be someone else and oh man that sounds like a lot of work.' But the reality is if we do not change we die as life is not possible without evolution.

We may find ourselves temporarily standing alone as we step away from people who may only be interested in offering friendship as long as we offer the same thoughts as them. Those who are close to us will provide us with the space to grow and those who are not will fade away. When we turn our energy away from our current circumstance, from things that are going wrong and people who are not in alignment with the expanded version of ourselves we make space for our reality to manifest. The feeling of isolation that may arise during this period will eventually dissipate as we master the relationship with our self and cultivate self-love that extends with a tentacular reach into our physical relationships. There is no need to expect anyone to change with or for us and there is no need for anyone to understand our decision to change; let them be. Our journey to inner transformation has everything to do with us and no one else.

We must be dogged with our intention to change and not let our awareness drift to aspects of our life we are unhappy with, as they will be transformed effortlessly. With patience, intention and consistency we will hit the point of no return and watch as the momentum of positive energy sweeps us off our feet. At times we may feel there is no end in sight but there will come a time when we can look back and observe how far we have come. The emotional breakdowns will have passed, we will have cried our tears, punched our pillows and declared we can longer live a small life that is fragile, unrewarding and conditional. It will feel like crossing a hump in the road, as we will have reconciled our trapped emotions, disposed of limiting thoughts and beliefs, and created space for a new way of being that allows miracles.

1.9 The tool of momentum

'Fear is always triggered by creativity, because creativity asks you to enter into realms of uncertain outcome, and fear hates uncertain outcome.'

- Elizabeth Gilbert

The world is always in flux. Nothing ever remains constant. We have talked a lot about change and how it affects us but what is the force behind it that allows us to follow through to an end result? The answer is momentum. Momentum is concentrated energy flowing in one direction and causing a repeated outcome. You might have heard the expression where focus goes energy flows, so when enough of our attention is flowing towards a particular person, circumstance or thought it becomes more powerful. What we focus on magnifies. Consistent focus on a circumstance perpetuates and solidifies the strength in momentum so much that we do not even have to work at it. Eventually the momentum graduates into a point of attraction that requires no effort to uphold and attracts experiences of a similar nature. When we are in the grips of negative momentum and try to counter the flow with a single happy thought it makes not even a mere indentation, as the flow will have taken on a life of its own. However, negative momentum is propelled by the emptiness of an illusion that only finds strength in fear. Once the illusion of separation has been reconciled the force of negative momentum dramatically reduces. Positive momentum is more durable as it is based in love not fear.

Imagine yourself white water rafting. The raging river you are paddling on is the momentum of your focus and the boat raft you are in is your thoughts. One day someone points out to you the direction your raft is headed and you decide you do not want to end up there, but the force of the river is so strong that even the thought of having to change terrifies you. You know it would be a lot easier to stay in your raft and remain ignorant of the destination but you do not want to end up there so you have got to change streams. Changing streams requires strong focus on where you want to go and developing the muscles that adjusts to a new river current. The fear mind says, 'well I've already developed the muscles to glide down this river so why would I want to get myself all wet? I may not like the end result but at least it's comfortable to me and I have experience dealing with these things.' The thought of change instigates an identity crisis and many people panic or remain ignorant because that is how they have been taught to manage adversity. When the momentum of negative emotion intensifies often we attach meaning to it and create an identity that requires these emotions to stay consistent. From this, experiences are drawn that elicit the same emotional responses and reaffirm the false identity.

Our source of love comes from our inner being but when we withhold it from ourselves with stories of lack or unworthiness we must look outside for it. That is when addictions form, as we must then attach ourselves to something or someone that fills the void. Toxic relationships also form when we expect someone to give us the love that can only be found within and exchanged between each other, not taken. Jealous relationships only survive when both parties lack self-love; one uses the other person as their source of love and the other person uses their neediness as their source of love. Someone who fills their own cup with love will not experience jealousy, as they know it is a tool of the fear mind that drains love. When we are in the stream of negative momentum it becomes a state of being that affects nearly every aspect of our life and is often seen as something to be resisted. However, resisting the flow is another fear response that assumes momentum is a form of punishment and that the universe does not support us, but it is in fact a tool we can use to create the life of our dreams without effort. When the weight of a raging river carries our raft it is near impossible to turn our weight against it so the way to change direction is to understand that momentum is an impartial tool of creation. Gratitude for the process of creation opens our mind up to seeing how the universe benefits us, not punishes us.

Accepting that all we think we are is merely a story we have created about repeated circumstances gives us the freedom to create our self anew by using momentum to guide us in the direction we want to go. Once we consistently flow our attention to what we want to experience, not the story of what is happening right now, creating the life of our dreams will become effortless. The work begins in believing in the benevolence of the universe and cultivating new beliefs that support a life of love, joy and abundance. Life is impartial to our decisions and will support all of our intentions no matter the outcome. It is always flowing energy towards love, as that is our natural state of being. Consistently envisioning and intending a life of greatness will invest power into that potential reality and expand its presence. When it grows big enough the universe aligns us with the potential reality through a path of least resistance, which usually occurs when we are doing something that centers our awareness on the present moment like walking, contemplation, showering, or exercising. When we make friends with momentum and see that it is here to serve us we can begin moving towards a life of greatness.

If we give less attention to the story about our circumstances and more attention to the infinite potential that exists in our imagination, less energy is expended recreating chronic negative experiences. Initially the shift will occur in our emotions as we notice a consistently improved mood. Emotional episodes will reduce in frequency and intensity, allowing joy to emerge. When the vibration of love and connection is practiced more often, joy becomes our natural emotional state and any emotion that counters it will be short-lived. Feelings of moving backwards will disappear and we will begin to see our goals reflected in those around us. Momentum will click into place and provide us with more thoughts, beliefs, emotions, people and experiences that match our new point of attraction so that it requires less conscious effort to maintain a higher vibration. Any experience that contradicts our new emotional state will be received as an opportunity to practice being in alignment with source. In time negative experiences will be seen for what they are; gifts of contrast.

1.10 The cause of suffering

'Nothing ever goes away until it teaches us what we need to know.'

- Pema Chödrön

Suffering is seen as an inherently negative experience endured by those who have sinned, which in the eyes of religion is everyone. It connotes an experience that brings about unnecessary emotional turmoil usually implemented by a higher power for its own selfish reasons to see humanity suffer. People ask, 'what kind of a God would allow such suffering to occur? How can a God have no sympathy for those in dire need of help? Doesn't he listen to our prayers?' Suffering is extreme resistance to our inner being. Our purpose on this planet is to embody the magnificence of all that we are through our experience on earth. This is a world of duality where one thing cannot exist without another; black needs white, light needs dark, up needs down, good needs bad and so on. In order to experience the fullness of who we are we need to experience the opposite of who we are and what better place to do it than in a world that allows suffering. In the non-physical there is no suffering or growth, there is only the absolute, which makes it impossible for the soul to know itself. To make it possible for growth there must exist an illusion of separation. The difference between temporary and long-term suffering is that one has a purpose and the other is self-inflicted.

Temporary suffering is an emotional reaction to a negative circumstance that is not trapped by identity, whereas long-term suffering can be endured for a lifetime and is often the result of momentum flowing in the direction of negative thought. If life were a canvas our thoughts would be paintbrushes and emotions our colours. If we paint a picture of life using the colour of suffering that is all we would see but if we paint it with the rosy complexion of love, oneness is all we would see. Suffering is a response to the misconception that we have been separated from source and we must spend our lives earning our way to heaven. In times of suffering there is no where to turn except inward and it is in these moments we discover that love is found within, not earned by a greedy God who plays favourites.

Diamonds are made under the pressure of mountains. When we fully experience the emotion of suffering whether through loss, addiction, depression, illness or heartache, the gift of finding our self becomes the sweetest reward. The point of every experience on earth is ultimately for us to experience our true nature and come home to source. Our inner being is always communicating with us, leaving breadcrumbs, whispering in our ear and leading us home. When we understand that believing in separation is pure insanity we can return to the heart of truth and end the need for suffering. Negative experiences will be seen as opportunities to grow and expand, not to prove our annihilation. We have been provided with the tools of creation; thought, emotion and momentum. In every moment we have the choice to use these tools to create a negative or a positive experience.

Let us examine the possible cause of suffering using the example of someone who has been struggling with depression for years. Author and motivational speaker Anthony Robbins discusses the blueprint we create for ourselves that outlines what we wish to experience and achieve in life. He says depression is a symptom of not fulfilling the blueprint and to remedy the situation we must either take action to fulfill it or change the blueprint. What makes people thrive is the feeling of growth and progress, which is a byproduct of setting a goal and successfully moving towards it. If we set a goal for our self that does not resonate with our purpose, or is created to satisfy superficial cravings or to please someone else we will feel the disparity between where we are and where we want to be. The enlightened person uses the negative emotion to reassess their vision whereas the victim uses the experience to perpetuate their story of suffering. The enlightened person is aware that life serves them and automatically identifies how the situation benefits them whereas the victim finds an excuse to remain the same.

For many people whose identity is rooted in victimhood extreme resistance is encountered during experiences that ask for change. When we experience extreme or chronic negative emotion it is an indication that we are not in alignment with what our inner being believes about us. Choosing to see how a situation can benefit us requires open-mindedness, a willingness to change and courage to see how we hold our self back from success. If we are willing to face our limiting beliefs we will have acquired a tool that can be used across the board. When we are in touch with our true nature and understand that life is nothing more than a physical manifestation of our thoughts we can move through difficult situations with ease. We can disassociate with the story behind the emotion and use our tools of creation to choose new thoughts that guide momentum in the direction we want to go. Instead of using the experience to think thoughts like, 'this always happens to me,' or, 'I am a failure,' we think thoughts that are more conducive to a positive inner mental state like, 'I am grateful for this experience showing me what beliefs are holding me back,' and, 'life is always on my side.'

If we remember that suffering is a great teacher we will have compassion for those suffering around us and be able to remain in the energy of love and appreciation. We will not look down on them with pity and nor will we join them in their suffering for we are now aware that out of great pressure comes great change. When we remain in the vicinity of love and joy we become an inspiration to many for we show them what is possible. When we say, 'poor you, you have it so tough,' we keep the suffering alive. It may feel difficult to maintain the feeling of joy when those close to us are suffering but ask yourself, if a friend is stuck in a well does it serve them for you to jump in with them? No, because in doing so we validate their story of victimhood but when we can hold the space for love we inadvertently remind them what their purpose is. Let us make this clear; life is not a struggle, we are not separate from the stream of wellbeing, and nor have we been condemned to a hell on earth by a jealous God. Everybody is born with their own inner being and no one has more access to 'the good stuff' than anyone else, it is simply about releasing our attachments and allowing in the stream that naturally flows to us. When we are open to the stream we are more able to inspire change in others as a manifestation of potential. We will need not to convince others to be like us or join us on our journey for they are free to act on their own. Judge not another person for where they are on their journey and the choices they have made for we are all doing our best with what we know.

1.11 Toxic people and behaviour

'If you truly loved yourself you would never hurt another.'

- Buddha

Once we move into a state of love we will begin to see evidence of the fear mind in its many cunning shapes. Fear can appear in many forms and often deceive those who are not strong enough in their vibration of self-love. Fear uses self-deprecating humour, jealousy, sexual allure, attention, showmanship and more to disguise and attract the attention of others. Some may attempt to reel us in with their tales of woe by implying that allowing us to hear them is a privileged look into their private lives. They may say things like, 'I don't share this with many people,' or, 'I've never told anyone this before but there is a reason I am the way I am. Listen to my justified story of fear that provokes pity so that when I hurt you, I can shirk ownership for my actions.' Some may pretend to be very guarded and attach themselves to people who are willing to offer consolation for their decision to remain in the fear mind.

As long as we are sympathetic to another's suffering we create space for it to exist. It serves no one to extend pity, consolation or even forgiveness for another's choice to remain unchanged. There is no such thing as a wrong deed, only an action that causes an outcome we choose to react to. It is important to understand that most people operate from the fear mind, some to a higher degree than others, and that we do not always need to take their actions personally. The drama of another person's life only affects us if we identify with their story of suffering. If we feel a negative emotion in response to the actions of another we are presented with the opportunity to remain centered in our vibration and make a decision. Forgiveness assumes that punishment and retribution exists. While it may be helpful in the process of healing from a traumatic event to experience the giving or receiving of forgiveness it is only a step on the emotional scale that eventually leads to liberation. True liberation occurs when we understand that in the eyes of source there is no wrongdoing, only actions that are not in alignment with love. People who are in the vicinity of love simply do not feel a compulsion to hurt themselves or another person.

Some people can be very charming in their ability to generate sympathy and once they have our vote will drain us of our sanity if we are not careful. They may attempt to seek attention by saying things like, 'I am a waste of air on this planet. Nobody likes me. I am always alone. Only you can understand me.' To which we will be expected to say, 'don't say that! You are an amazing person and everybody loves you.' This only feeds their ego and keeps them from seeing the reality of their behaviour. If we confront them about their behaviour they may attempt to use guilt as a means of justification and any attempt to change them will prove futile. It is not our responsibility to change another person or convince them of their worth. Everyone has their own inner being guiding them back to source, which they can choose to listen to or ignore. As we have discovered, toxic behaviour is a byproduct of lack of self-love, which we can only help others to feel when we are open to the stream of wellbeing that fills our own cup with love. Relying on another's emotional state to remain constant to ease our worries helps no one. When we are grounded in our connection to source it is impossible to be drained by another.

If a person of this nature has affected you know they are trapped in a hell of their own making. When we are in tune with our own source we are more capable of deflecting these people as they will sense our strength and move on. Rest in the knowingness that this type of person will only stick around as long as we give them our sympathy. Needing constant reassurance of our appearance, of our self worth or of our sense of humour is a quality that can only be reciprocated by those of similar nature. The enlightened person needs nothing from another and expresses every action from the vibration of love. What is holding you back from totally loving yourself? What is holding you back from letting go of the need for approval from others? What thoughts and beliefs are resisting the stream of wellbeing? Release your friends and loved ones from the responsibility of maintaining your emotional wellbeing and release yourself of the burden of maintaining another's. The only person who can cultivate inner peace is you.

Spend time in contemplation and resist the urge to throw up a smoke screen by jumping into relationships or looking for more people to leech attention from. Contemplate the true source of love and whether we truly need the sympathy of others to feel validated. Imagine how many people would rave about our company if we were connected to our own stream of wellbeing. We would be so full to the brim with love that we would require nothing from anyone. We would be a pure joy to be around and we will have fulfilled our purpose of experiencing who we really are. Our old ways of managing the feeling of inadequacy will no longer satisfy us because we will have finally realised we were looking for love in all the wrong places. Love does not come from another; it is exchanged between the two so neither is in debt. It is our responsibility to show up for ourselves, and thank God for that, because nobody can be us better than ourselves.

If everything in life is temporary then so too is suffering. It is as the Persian adage goes; *and this, too, shall pass away.* The world is constant flux, changing with new ideas, new thoughts, and new ways of being. Impermanence is the foundation of life for it brings growth and exploration. Without it we would remain stagnant and life would become very humdrum. If we were to only eat our favourite fruit for the rest of our time on this planet we would grow to dislike it because we are evolutionary creatures always finding ways to adapt and better ourselves. Variety is the spice of life. Our bodies thrive off the different summation of nutrients found in different foods and the same goes for our experience in life.

People who truly love and support us want us to succeed on our journey of inner transformation. Our reason for change must come from a selfish place of wanting to be so full of love that we have enough to share with others. The key to successful relationships is to bring love to the table, not problems. Our partners want to see us succeed and will rejoice with us through all the ups and downs. If we put pressure on another to fill the void of our own inadequacy it will only spell drama and dissatisfaction. We can enhance the quality of our relationships by changing your perspective from 'what can I take?' to, 'what can I give?'

1.12 Understanding depression

'Feel what you need to feel then let it go. Do not let it consume you.'

- Ishwar Dass Dhiman

Emotions filter how much joy we allow into our lives. Joy is our natural state of being that is sometimes blocked with negative emotion like guilt, shame, hate or blame. Each negative emotion possesses a different quality that makes us look at the world from a different perspective, for example, depression makes the world feel heavy and uninviting whereas anxiety makes the world feel like a threat. Depending on how strong the emotion is it can change not just our perception but also our personality. It becomes a quality that dictates our actions, guides our thoughts and restricts what we allow ourselves to experience. People who live in states of depression often refer to it as a friend because it poses as a source of comfort. It is always there for them when others let them down. We grow accustomed to certain emotions because we are familiar with the actions and thoughts associated with the feeling. When we identify with an emotion and create a story about it we create an addiction that supports the identity of the small self.

Despite the improvement of healthcare systems and enhancements of anti-depressant drugs, rates of depression continue to surge. With more people living a sedentary lifestyle we are no longer exposed to the everyday challenges that strengthen our ability to adapt to stress or provide us with a sense of accomplishment. In the western world acquiring basic needs is as easy as driving to the supermarket or turning on the heater. Less exposure to stress means that when we face stressful circumstance in our personal lives we are unequipped at taking appropriate action and solving problems. Those who refrain from partaking in regular physical exercise also produce smaller doses of serotonin in the brain, a hormone that promotes happiness and wellbeing. When we are consistently in the vicinity of appreciation we are more easily able to process stress response chemicals like dopamine and epinephrine that can linger in the body if not properly expressed.

If left untreated these lingering emotions can elevate into a state of being that influences the body to live in a perpetual state of stress. Depression manifests when we feel powerless to the circumstance and unmotivated by the end result. To alleviate the intensity of depression it is useful to reassess the purpose of one's life so that it is more achievable and rewarding. An often overlooked and undervalued goal is to feel good. To some it may appear fickle or undesirable on their quest for fame, fortune or power, thinking that once they attain a specific outcome they can then allow themselves to feel happy. But success is nothing if the journey is not enjoyed. It can be said that those experiencing depression are at an advantage because they must look within to find pleasure and purpose, which so many fail to do so. Depression is not lifted by the temptations of the physical world. We must seek for a deeper reward, which is a return to source.

In many cases the host personifies the feeling of depression so that it takes on a comforting nature. In the song, *The Sound of Silence,* Simon and Garfunkel sing, 'hello darkness my old friend, I've come to talk with you again.' This is nothing more than the fear mind taking pleasure in old habits that produce familiar outcomes that validate and perpetuate its existence. Depression is often seen as an emotional state to be resisted but if we ask an empowering question we can begin the process of breaking our attachment to suffering. Instead of asking, 'why me? How can I get rid of this feeling? What is wrong with me?' we could ask, 'what is the message trying to emerge behind the pain?' This immediately transforms our way of thinking away from victimhood and into love. Depression is an opportunity to turn over the stone of the soul and admire another of its facets. While it is a symptom of disconnection with source it is also, paradoxically, the solution to ending the illusion of disconnection.

To be eternally free of depression one has to recognise that the thoughts they think do not allow joy. The moment we consciously redirect our thoughts to where we want to go life immediately meets us. We begin with identifying the sponsoring thought behind the depression and ask empowering questions that change our state from powerlessness to hope. Through deep inner inquiry we ask ourselves why we feel depressed and our response may be 'nothing motivates me.' The mind may create a story such as, 'I am old, I am unlucky in love, I despise my job, my purpose alludes me and I see no point in trying,' etc. This may express an emotion but the sponsoring thought is one of inadequacy. Empowering questions we can ask about depression include:

- Are my circumstances the only indication of my worthiness?
- What if everything is working out for me even though it seems like it isn't?
- What if this is the perfect opportunity to reinvent myself and discover what I really like to do?
- What if the people around me will support and help me in my quest to discover my purpose?
- What would happen if I opened myself up to new possibilities?
- What if this depression is simply indicating to me that I need to make some changes?'

Remember, the obstacle is the way. Rather than wrestling with the depression, we listen to its message and make the adjustments necessary in our life to allow in more joy. Every emotion of resistance communicates to us that change needs to be made to our thoughts, habits and actions. Depression asks us to look at our source of pain and give it love. When we make it our intention to feel good no matter the circumstance our inner being will guide us to the right books, films, songs and teachers that propel us in the direction of our vision. When we make a clear intention to the universe it will without fail provide us with everything we need to accomplish the task. Louise Hay states in her book *You Can Heal Your Life* that all ailments and issues come down to lack of self-love. When we face difficult circumstances it is life's way of inviting us to love ourselves more. Depression can make us feel like a failure but if we could see ourselves from source's perspective we would see how much we are adored. This is our life and only we can decide whether we want to live in pain or harmony.

Depressive states can feel very heavy and difficult to move through. Not only does it appear impossible to feel better, we simply do not see the point in feeling good. When a depressive episode strikes and we feel like we cannot break free the easiest way to approach it is to allow the experience to occur, remain free of judgment, and do something to take our mind off it. Sitting at home, watching television or lying in bed with our thoughts will likely prolong suffering, as the mind will use the quietude to convince us of its story. Remember the thoughts that arise in the experience are just that; thoughts. It is our job to relax, breath, remain open and direct our attention to a place that feels good even if we do not want to. Go for a walk, move the body, meet with a friend, read a book in the sun, buy a croissant at the local bakery, have a picnic in the park, do anything that diverts attention away from what is and into the deliciousness of the present moment.

When we feel bliss we are too absorbed in the here and now to ask questions like, 'who am I?' or, 'why am I here?' Clarity arrives in a state of pleasure. Every person's basic need and desire is to feel like its true self and depression can be an excellent tool for helping us to look inside and find connection with source. Depression holds everything we think we know about life in suspension so we can observe it and ask if it is really true. We will know we are connected with source when we feel joyful, liberated, clear and free. The changes we need to make will become clear and we will begin moving in the right direction. Trying to change our external reality without changing the inner world is like trying to change the clothes in the mirror and not the body. The world is nothing more than a reflection of our thoughts so if there is something occurring in our lives that we dislike we must change our internal world. The universe is at our service and whatever we demand from it we will receive so it is up to us to ask for something that benefits us.

Learning to ask empowering questions is the key to uncovering our purpose and to creating a desirable experience for our time here on earth. The more disempowering questions we ask the more negative experiences we have and the more depressed we feel. Our soul instills within us a purpose that it intends to fulfill, and if the body passes before that purpose is fulfilled it will continue into the next life. Suicide solves no problems except to temporarily relieve suffering in a personal hell. While there is no shame in those who have chosen to take their lives, they have unfortunately missed out on the experience of rising from the bottom. We do not have to die to experience heaven on earth. There is no satisfaction like hitting rock bottom and using the experience to create a new vision.

When we hit the point of no return momentum swings in our favour and the river of life takes us in the direction of joy simply because our thoughts are focused away from current circumstance and onto new thoughts that reflect the desired experience. Awareness expands from the small self to a new creative state of being more conducive to allowing joy. Once we begin to realise we are the creator of our reality and understand how we mold our physical experience life becomes fun and interesting. We are no longer able to hold others responsible for the way we feel and we longer feel the need to wallow in sadness when things do not go our way, for we understand that everything is temporary, stories are illusions, and life is supposed to be fun. In the outside world people will respond differently to our new vibration and new experiences will match our new state of being. When we reach this place we will look back on our time of depression with gratitude because it gave us the key to our destiny.

1.13 Understanding anxiety

'The art of living lies less in eliminating your troubles than it does in growing with them.'

- Bernard Baruch

Anxiety is an emotional state of being derived from the flight or fight stress hormone that triggers feelings of worry, stress, apprehension, and tension. It is the body's way of responding to a possible threat supporting alertness and quick decisions. People living in dangerous neighbourhoods or abusive relationships possess high levels of cortisol due to the constant possible threat of physical danger, causing them to live in a higher state of arousal than most. In other cases people who experience traumatic events often internalise the experience so that the mind falsely believes it is in constant danger. If the emotion behind the trauma is stored for a prolonged period of time the trapped emotion is expressed as a physical ailment, ranging from premature grey hairs to cancer. Whether the threat is real or imaginary, present or past, the body reacts to the threat as if it were happening in real time, thus motivating habits that respond to stress. Panic attacks occur at random, unexpected times and often compliment symptoms of depression. Those who suffer from panic attacks live in a constant state of fear. Panic disorder is experienced as an over stimulation of chemicals in the brain causing feelings of lightheadedness, queasiness, shortness of breath, sudden alertness, and cessation of the digestive system. From the perspective of the mind it feels like something is going very wrong and the body is in extreme danger. Panic attacks are a very frustrating experience that limit what the person is comfortable doing and can occur at random. Ways of dealing with panic include drug and alcohol abuse, emotional withdrawal and even suicide. Suicide is often symbiotic with depression because it seems like the easiest way to escape pain that is eternal and unforgiving.

Anxiety is usually stimulated by an emotional response that was once triggered during a previously stressful event. As a way of protecting itself against a repeated outcome, the mind releases the stress hormones as if it were happening in the current moment. For example, a child accidentally locked in the bathroom by a parent will internalise the event as trauma. Feelings associated with the event may include panic, entrapment and abandonment. The child being underdeveloped in its emotional capacity to deal with the event stores the emotion in the body until later. The trapped energy can manifest itself again in future events that result in a similar outcome. Twenty years later the same person may feel a sense of unease catching public transport as it triggers the feeling of entrapment. If the same emotion of entrapment is felt it can trigger physiological responses such as tension, shortness of breath, increased heartbeat and panic attacks. An experience that may seem unrelated is actually very strongly correlated. The way we attach meanings to physical sensations strongly influences our response to certain physiological responses; for example, shortness of breath and rapid heartbeat can be associated with an orgasm as well as a panic attack.

Anxiety is an emotion that carries its own distinct way of expressing resistance to our wellbeing. It differs from depression in that it stimulates alertness rather than oppression but just like with any emotion it is triggered by a thought. Remember that if a feeling is just a thought, a thought can be changed. A panic attack is an extreme reaction to a perceived threat. When it takes over the body there is not much that can be done except to endure and recover. The key to releasing anxiety is just the same as with any other emotion; identifying the sponsoring thought, feeling the emotion and changing the thought so that momentum can flow in the direction we want to go. What is the feeling that triggers panic? What were we thinking about before the attack came on? Where were we? What were we doing? It all begins by recognising we are not our thoughts but the observer who possesses the power to create the life we desire. With strong intention and passion for the vision anything is possible. To begin shifting the momentum ask this question, 'what kind of thoughts would I think if I lived life free of anxiety?' We might think thoughts like:

- I am comfortable trying new experiences
- I feel safe and secure everywhere I go
- Life has my back
- I am loved and supported
- I love and approve of myself
- I am relaxed and at ease
- Feelings are just thoughts and thoughts can be changed
- Life is my friend
- Life adores me
- I am connected to my inner being
- I love all that I've been and all that I am becoming
- I am moving towards love
- All is well in my world
- I am in the rhythm and flow of life

We do not have to immediately believe these thoughts, just feel the energy behind them as opposed to thoughts of panic. Writing them down on a piece of paper and referring to them throughout the day can assist in changing our mind so that safety becomes our new normal. Anxiety is nothing more than a habit of thought and if we change the thought we can create a new habit that encourages an inner world of love and peace. Consistently repeating these phrases imbues a feeling of safety that will in time evolve into a belief. Deep breathing and learning to self soothe is an invaluable tool that can be used to counter any negative emotion not just limited to anxiety. We have nothing to fear but fear it self. The only thing standing in the way between where we are and where we want to be is the fear of being unloved, and once we reconcile with this delusion we will require nothing from anybody. There is no joy in the illusion of separation; the seeker can only become a finder once they realise they are the one causing the seeking. In the book *Four Agreements,* author Don Miguel Ruiz says always do your best for when you do there is nothing to criticise, only to improve and compliment.

1.14 Guilt as self-punishment

'When we deny the story, it defines us. When we own the story, we can write a brave new ending.'

- Brené Brown

Guilt is a form of self-punishment derived from the illusion of inadequacy that deflects our stream of wellbeing and prevents us from embracing our potential. It infers that something has gone wrong and we must be punished. While some may believe self-punishment makes us worthy of reclaiming our right to joy it actually prolongs suffering and causes us to hurt others. A person who is hurt usually inadvertently seeks to hurt another to fill the gap they have created for themselves. For example, a man cheats on his wife in the belief that his happiness lies in the hands of his mistress. The new relationship fails because the guilt of tearing apart his marriage disallows him from permitting himself to love. The first mistake was assuming his wife was the sponsoring cause of unhappiness and the second was not forgiving himself for the mistake. *A Course in Miracles* states we are never upset for the reason we think we are. If we believe our happiness lies in the eradication or transformation of an external stimulus then it is likely it exists in our experience as an invitation to turn inwards.

Giving ourselves permission to make mistakes allows us to learn and evolve so that we can make new decisions that elevate our consciousness. Choosing to wallow in guilt and self-pity serves nobody as it maintains the momentum of suffering. Only when we choose to love can we make decisions that bring about joy and peace. Contrast is the illusion of duality that exists for us to discover who are by discovering who we are not. Using this tool we can decipher what we want from what we do not want but if our identity takes the contrast personally we will continue to hold ourselves apart from wellbeing.

When we live outside of the present moment we construct a perception of reality that is borrowed from opinions of past experiences. When we live in a state of guilt and shame we create experiences that reflect back to us these emotions, therefore confirming our belief that we deserve punishment. The only way to break the cycle is to become aware of the fallacy we are anything other than love and choose to believe in something new. There is no law that states we must continue to think as we always have. We have the freedom right now to choose love.

It is everybody's inherent right to experience joy. If we are stuck believing that those who have done wrong deserve to be unhappy it is only an indicator that we too believe we must be punished. Only those who love can see that the answer to every problem is more love. Guilt and shame are traits passed down by a generation whose beliefs were shaped by several bouts of global turmoil including two world wars, a great depression, a missile crisis, a mass genocide, ongoing struggles with racism and sexism, etc. all caused by these emotions. Memorials have been erected to remind ourselves daily of the struggle we have endured without realising that the more attention we flow to injustice the more it is perpetuated. No wonder it is difficult for many to envision new and exciting ways of transforming pain into opportunity. Identifying contrast is essential to growth but peace must be made with the past if we are to envision a new life of unity and joy.

For example a shift worker has a negative experience with a customer at work and tells their partner about the experience. Venting can be a temporarily beneficial tool that assists in identifying the cause of pain and releasing trapped emotion, thus allowing the worker to encounter positive interactions with customers in the future. However, if the worker elevates the pain of the negative interaction with a story about how they are always at the mercy of customers in bad moods and that the politics of retail is corrupt, they become a victim to their own story of reality. This is equivalent to building a statue in commemoration of a negative experience. Life is calling us to more elevated states of love and joy but if we constantly activate the story of victimhood we do not see the possibilities of what could be. It is our responsibility to clear the shame and guilt that traps us in victimhood and choose to return to love. Only when this is achieved can we envision a life of new possibilities and follow through on it. When we thank life for providing us with the opportunity to become aware of our pain we can shift our attention away from current reality and onto the potential for love.

PART TWO

Transformation Of The Outer World

'Potential is always bigger than the problem. Your potential is infinite and is always bigger than whatever problem you're going through. And your life begins to be okay when you wake up in the morning and say, 'I'm going to walk in the direction of my purpose. I'm going to walk in the direction of my vision.' You're being pulled more by joy… Talk to the possibility. Talk to love. You talk to peace. You talk to it. And then after a while, you're talking *from* it.'

Michael Bernard Beckwith

2.1 The power of intention

'Happiness is not found in the things you possess, but in what you have the courage to release.'

- Nathaniel Hawthorne

The most powerful initiator of change is intending for things to be different. When a statement is made to the universe that we expect change and are willing to take the necessary action to implement it, victim energy is counteracted with power. We retract power from external circumstances and instead focus on cultivating an inner world that flourishes with love and abundance. Once we take our power back from the outside world our work shifts from maintaining order to clearing the pathway for experiences that deliver the fullness of who we are. Only when we transform limiting beliefs and open the window for refreshing ideas can we experience the potential for greatness that is always available to us.

The universe is a field of energy that communicates to us our dominant vibration through reflection of thoughts, which is then felt as emotion. Physical reality causes us to feel emotion that demands to be felt and helps us to make sense of the world, for without them life would be meaningless and we would never experience growth. Negative emotion is interpretation of disparity between what we are thinking and what source is thinking. Negative emotions feel unpleasant because they are not in conjunction with our natural state of oneness and slow down the flow of wellbeing. Positive emotions feel pleasant because they vibrate at higher frequencies that are in alignment with source. When we are experiencing unfavorable circumstances and consistent negative emotions it is simply the universe's way of showing to us that a change needs to be made if we are to step into greatness. If we ignore the call and continue to react as we always have, we create negative momentum that perpetuates the manifestation of unpleasant circumstances and emotional reactions.

When this occurs we can either accept the negative momentum as a way of life or wait until the separation from source becomes so unbearable we pop. Popping is an unofficial, unscientific yet completely relatable term used to describe the experience of hitting breaking point. When momentum is strongly flowing in the direction of what we do not want and negative emotion builds, our extreme rejection of the experience causes friction so strong we burst free. Usually it compels people to say things like, 'that's it! I can't take it anymore,' or, 'I'm so sick of the way things are, I need to change,' or, 'surely there is more to life than this.' The power of intention in that moment is so strong it immediately starts flowing energy in the opposite direction. Then we go on to say, 'things need to change. Surely I'm not living to my full potential and life has more to offer than this. I'm ready to do whatever it takes to change and live a better life. I know in my heart there is more and I intend to find it!'

In the instant we intend to live a better life our identification with negative thinking habits weaken and space is created for new ways of being that are more conducive for positive emotion. With consistent repetition of new thoughts we build new neural pathways that support our new way of thinking. Strong intention is a very effective way of swinging momentum in another direction, but without reaffirmation the power will wither and the old momentum will quickly swing back into effect rendering our efforts ineffective. It is important to remain focused on our desire for better and choose it everyday like we are choosing it for the first time. The public speaker that leads with passion and purpose is more effective at recruiting momentum than the competitor who speaks quietly and without conviction. Strong intention sends out a flare signal for greatness to find them, which is immediately met with new thoughts that expect us to grow into the person we wish to embody. In an age of fear we must be prepared to think differently than most and we can do that together.

2.2 Applying change

'I think the truth is if you really care about the quality of somebody's life as much as your own you have truly made it.'

- Edie Windsor

During our time of inner transformation we can use our physical reality as a tool to loosely quantify how much we have changed. We can place identification on circumstance and exert an emotional reaction or we can remain unaffected. If we feel an impulse to react negatively we will see our attachment to the small self but if we choose to remain the observer and release our attachment to fear we will know we have changed. We cannot always control every circumstance that passes through our experience and nor will they always be pleasant but we do have power over our reaction and overall vision. When we transform our inner world so that our point of attraction is elevated we attract and become attracted to people and experiences of an elevated nature. Negative emotions will not be as intense or sustained and those that are not in harmony with our state of being will not prey on us for consolation. Replacing sympathy with empathy gives others the chance to grow without needing to drag others down.

It is likely that with our newly curated mindset we will see in others who we once were and feel shocked at how many people live in fear, even those who seem to have it all. People, places or habits once found irresistible will become repulsive as greatness becomes the new normal. This is common amongst former addicts who no longer find short-term gratification in old habits and connection with like-minded addicts. For many this causes a significant shift in every aspect of their lives including living conditions, employment, relationships and physical health, which can take some time to adjust to. Recognise that outgrowing the life we once accepted as normal is a sign of growth and that new experiences await. Friends or work colleagues will wonder what has changed and may even ask what is 'wrong.' They may say, 'what is wrong with you? You seem different. You don't seem like your normal self.' Or they may simply drop out of awareness if the manifestation of greatness is too intimidating to accept. The opinions of those who do not support us are derived from fear and affect us not for we are driven by our vision for greatness.

Keep in mind that feeling superior to those still living in fear is a sign we have not grown as dominance is born of insecurity, so have compassion and give them no mind. Everybody is living their life the best they can based on what they have learnt from the opinions of others and their past experiences. When we come to grasp how many people live in fear we can extend compassion and retract our identity from the actions of others as we transform our own limiting beliefs. The enlightened person takes responsibility for their thoughts and doggedly teaches themselves new ways of being without being persuaded by fear. The way we can guide others to follow their own truth is by being our whole and complete self. Great masters understand that the best gift we can give others is the ability to be oneself. Allow others to feel safe being their true selves in our presence and we will inspire a desire in them to recognise their full potential.

The best gift we can give the world is our best self, not a second rate version of someone else. Embodying our greatest self requires intuition, patience, intention and persistence. This is not to be mistaken with being happy all the time or being vulnerable with everyone. Stepping forward as our true authentic self gives others permission to do so as well. When we make it a safe space to allow emotion to pass through without judgment including shame, embarrassment, guilt, resentment and anger we inadvertently encourage change in others by showing that it is safe to do so for themselves. They will see the change in us and wish to replicate it in themselves for we have shown that it is possible to live a life of greatness. This is our chance to tell our own rags to riches story.

The Buddha says all suffering comes from unsatisfied desire; so we can either change the desire or fulfill it. There is immense satisfaction that comes from watching our world change from the inside out. The first sign of change manifests in an improved mood. Chronic negative emotions weaken in intensity and longevity, and positive emotions begin to surface with more consistency. This occurs when we process blocked emotions, access the source of power within and set powerful intentions of change. We begin to have new ideas and new impulses that establish new thought patterns and allow in new opportunities. Once joy, empowerment, love and connection become our new state of being those changes are reflected in the outside world and anyone who is not in support of our vision will leave. If a negative experience arises we are more equipped at detaching from the outcome and appreciating the process. Eventually we will be so drawn by our vision that the temptation to return to old habits will dissipate and those around us will look on in amazement at the courage it took to step into greatness.

2.3 Embracing the fluidity of identity

'Others have seen what is and asked why. I have seen what could be and asked why not.'

- Pablo Picasso

Identity is our physical form of self-expression. It is the story we create about ourselves based on past experiences and why we are the way we are. We can use it to justify our behaviour, for example, a person who hurts others may say, 'I do these things because my father abused me as a child and I don't know any other way to cope with my emotions,' or, 'my previous lovers really hurt me so I'm going to hurt you first to protect myself from being hurt again.' Identities help us make sense of the world and carve our place in it so we feel like we have a purpose. Instead of remaining the observer and allowing experiences to pass through without attachment, our identity, sometimes referred to as the ego or small self, takes it personally. It asks questions like:

- Why did this happen?
- What is my place in this?
- How does this fit into my story about who I am?
- How can I make this about me?

Internalisation can only borrow answers that come from old patterns of thinking and memories of previous experiences, leaving no room for inspiration or new ways of thinking. Identity can be a fun tool to play with but when taken personally or identified with too strongly it clouds our perception and restricts the fluidity of reality. We have several identities that we switch between throughout the day, for example, we can be a mother, a tennis player, a student, a friend, a wife, a mistress, a daughter, a bartender and with each role we show a different face, so why do we become attached to roles that cause pain? Why get stuck playing the role of the girl with 'daddy issues,' or the one who only knows poverty when we can be anything we choose? This is a world of limitless potential and we can explore whatever role we wish to play. In the script of your life ask these questions:

- What character do I want to play?
- What thoughts and beliefs does my character think?
- Is there someone I can look up to who already embodies this identity?
- What would it mean for me to identify as someone who is successful?
- What does my character associate success with?
- What would she/he do if they were in my position?
- What kind of thoughts and beliefs does she/he identify with?
- How does she/he sound when he interacts with others?

Perhaps you have always wanted to write a book but your current identity throws up excuses that dissuade you from achieving your goal. Borrowing advice from past experiences and opinions of others will get us nowhere but if we ask creative questions that cause us to think of answers we have never thought of before we break attachment to the fear mind. Attempting to combat the voice of limitation with amorphous goals will prove futile so it is in our best interest to ask questions that stimulate creativity. Depending on how strong the fear is we may not immediately conjure a new identity but creative curiosity will gently encourage inner change. Let us not get carried away with specific details about time, money, and feasibility, as when we are stuck in our old identity we will not be open to receiving empowering solutions. Instead, ask general questions like:

- I may not know the answers yet but what if it were possible?
- What if the answer is just around the corner?
- What if the universe orchestrated this experience so I would ask these questions?

- If I could open myself up to the stream of wellbeing what kind of ideas could I receive?
- How can I direct my focus so that I can believe it's possible?

Then our mind will start firing off new brain wires in all different directions, finding memories that support success and discovering thoughts that make the idea seem possible. There is a period of adjustment that takes place as the brain weakens old patterns of thinking and strengthens new neural pathways. Temporary relapses are inevitable and vital to progression but to prevent permanent reversion to old, limiting habits we must consistently reaffirm our vision. Choosing to change is a brave and courageous feat that can make us feel like everything has been thrown up in the air but eventually the dust will settle. It will be easier to resist the urge to think old thoughts when we take time to imagine what our new life will feel like. Inner transformation is not always smooth sailing and can be a confronting experience if we are deeply imbedded in the identity of a close minded thinker but once we see the change we are making we will feel compelled to continue showing up. Soon enough momentum will flip and it will feel natural to identify as the one who was courageous enough to confront their dark side in search for the light. Not everyone chooses this road but we have and these are the tools that will help us see it through. Have appreciation for your decision to change and live a better life.

When we encounter a negative experience it is easy to ask why it happened to us and what we did to deserve it, but if the universe supports us in our growth then we must ask how the experience benefits us. As we have discovered the universe communicates to us our point of attraction by way of physical experience and our emotional reaction to it. There is no need to identify with the experience or take it personally as it is merely a reflection of our inner world. If our natural state of being is joy, love and inner peace, anything other than those is an indicator that something is blocking us from reaching our full potential. When faced with a negative experience we have the choice to transform and transcend the situation. Transformation involves turning weaknesses into strengths, using the alchemy of the universe to turn a negative into a positive. We transform a situation when we completely heal the sponsoring emotion and are able to see the beauty in it. Some people refer to it as a blessing in disguise. An example may be getting fired from a job you were comfortable in but using the opportunity to reassess your life's direction and get a new job that uplifts you. Transcendence occurs when we no longer attach ourselves to the situation and it eventually transforms into something beautiful.

2.4 Knowing when to take action

'You have to keep breaking your heart until it opens.'

-Rumi

The process of change involves 90% inner work and 10% action. In fact, the majority of action we take is changing our inner world and the rest is responding to prompts the universe gives us. When we take on the task of transformation we naturally decipher what we want from what we do not want. The new experiences and things we wish to receive becomes a potential reality in the field of the cosmos, which is accessible only by clearing the emotional pathway to our stream of wellbeing. Sustained focus on our current reality indicates we have attached meaning to the meaningless and have lost sight of our truth. Author Esther Hicks says in her book *Ask and it is Given* that when we are shouting 'no' at something we are actually shouting 'yes' at it because attention expands what we focus on. If we are driving in a slow lane it does not serve us to find ways to speed up that lane, we must change lanes. Our current reality is not a definitive guide for what is possible.

Chronic negative circumstances are a product of consistently focusing attention on negative emotional reactions. Feeling stuck is an illusion because nothing is constant; we are simply recreating the same experience over and over again by choosing to focus our awareness on negative emotion when in fact the opportunity to create something new exists in every moment. The power we have is in the choices we make now. We are not the summation of our previous choices or experiences, we are the person we choose to be in the moment, and when we choose to be the person we want to be enough times and with enough conviction, momentum creates circumstance that reflect our new identity. It begins with an intention, which then snowballs into a deed, which is then repeated enough times until finally an identity is formed. The power comes when we can see what we dislike in our experience, declare that is not who we are and choose to change the story we have fabricated in response to it. There is no need to condemn the story for it was designed to protect us from exploring the pain that resides in our subconscious, but when we come to realise love is our natural state of being all fear dissipates for darkness cannot exist in the presence of light.

A common though unnatural way of coping with change is to lean on addictions, call the person we know will not help us and avoid the process until hopefully something shifts on its own. This kind of resistance to change occurs when we notice an emotional imbalance within and seek to fill the void outside ourselves. Even those who try to find themselves through religion or spirit can get stuck 'seeking' as they attempt to identify with an outside source for validation. Yet one cannot see what they are, only a reflection of it. Eventually we all come to realise our source of love comes from within or that which cannot be seen. Those stuck in fear tend to think about the situation that triggered change in the first place, use the person who hurt them as an excuse to prolong the illusion of separation and think of solutions to fix it. Disempowering questions may drift into their awareness like, 'what did I do wrong? How can I fix this? How can I change the other person?' However, if we are feeling off about something in our life that is simply an indicator that the way we see it is off.

Action inspired by fear, not love, is an invitation for pain and suffering. If we shift our perspective from, 'why is this happening to me?' to, 'how can I use this for my growth?' we are more conducive to ideas that bring about positive change. Negative emotion such as revenge, dissatisfaction, or contempt can be an effective tool for initiating inner transformation but will need to evolve if it is to be sustained. When love becomes the driver of motivation we take action because we feel inspired, not because we need to. If an opportunity or an idea arises that inspires doubt, uncertainty or unease it may be the fear mind attempting to solve an issue out of desperation or impatience. In this case it is better to more clearly refine the desire, recognise the never ending stream of opportunities and trust that when we come into alignment with our stream of wellbeing we will encounter ideas for action that create positive and long lasting change. Get comfortable with unresolved desire and enjoy the experience of watching desire unfold. Life is a circulation of push and pull, dreaming and creating. There is a time for action and a time for imagining, and when the opportunities presented are not wanted, pull back and keeping envisioning the new life. More ideas will flow, what we want will become clearer and we will have a better understanding of what lies ahead. It is like feeling around for something in the dark or searching with a blindfold; we cannot see what we are looking for, we must feel our way there. We will feel closer to it when the idea or potential experience excites us, ignites passion and makes us feel inspired. It will feel like the right thing to do.

When we enjoy the process of manifestation we give ourselves permission to feel joy right now, not just when the desire arrives. Eventually we will look back on our experience with reverence and appreciation because if it were not for the negative experiences we would never have realised our full potential. Daydreaming is an extremely beneficial tool that allows us to uncover hidden thoughts and ideas without the threat of analysis or criticism. When we daydream thoughts pass like waves in the ocean of consciousness without attachment and we are free to build any kind of life we desire. In our imagination we can envision fulfilling our desire for revenge or our desire for indulgence. It gives us the freedom to explore our emotions and move through them once it becomes clear what the true desire is. A desire for revenge is a desire for love. A desire to quit a job is a desire for freedom. A desire to rob a bank is a desire for power. While people may ask for different things the underlying desires are the same; we all want love, freedom, growth, joy and connection. Any kind of pain is a disconnection from source.

2.5 Accepting where we are

'Self-care is giving the world the best of you, instead of what's left of you.'

- Katie Reed

There is a distinct difference between admitting where we are versus continuously talking about where we are. Accepting where we are involves having the courage to put down our pitchfork and admitting things could be better whereas continuously talking about it encourages powerlessness. This state of emotion usually compels people to give their power away by recruiting an audience for their drama, which acts as a smokescreen for their true emotions. True acceptance is a noble feat that can be difficult for some to achieve if their emotion has evolved into a state of being. Acceptance can be brought about by recognising that change is possible, and we have permission to feel what we are feeling. Resisting the truth is futile and inhibits our growth. This can be difficult to do in a world where depression is romanced and so many of us do not possess the knowledge we need to change. Many of us still live under the illusion that life is happening to us not through us.

There is even some confusion in the self-help movement that implies feeling angry or vengeful is not spiritual, but if everything is derived from the divine then there is nothing that cannot be spiritual. Some texts even imply the act of desiring affirms to the universe that we are not supported, which is met with more longing. Yet desire is a natural process that is meant to inspire and expand the mind, but this can be countered by desperation if it is believed we must struggle to have our needs met. To desire something is not bad, it is a natural response to situations that provide us with contrast or lack. It is an excellent tool that allows us to refine what we want and take action that reflects the change we wish to see. Continuously talking about the things we want in a manner that makes us feel hopeless or uninspired inhibits our ability to come into alignment with our inner being whereas acceptance gives us space to focus on what we want. It is safe to admit the truth about how we feel, that perhaps we are not living our dream life, that we are not over the pain of a breakup, that something affected us more than we anticipated, that we dislike someone's actions, that the person who got the promotion over us was undeserving, or whatever it may be. Make it a safe environment for you to confide in yourself.

There may be others in our life that will support us but keep in mind that every one possesses opinions based on their understanding of what they think is best and may not always be relevant to us. Admitting the truth is not admitting defeat; it is coming into contact with our power to change. Accepting the truth about how we feel dissipates any feelings of hostility, anger or frustration towards the way things are and allows us to cultivate a more creative platform for us to imagine what we wish to experience. Rather than hopelessly shouting 'why me?' to the heavens we can say, 'what can I do to change?' The power comes back to us and from this new standpoint we can get the universe to work for us.

Religion has an exponential impact on the way we view the world and our position in it. If we think of God as our father in heaven we think of a man who owns our lives. If we want something we must ask permission, if we do something wrong we must repent, and if we dare ask for help we must sacrifice something in return. But what if we could see God as our best friend? It might be a far cry for some religions to shift their perception but what would it mean if he were our best friend as opposed to a dominating father figure? Best friends entail symbiosis and a circulation of give and take rather than worshipping. When one is in need the other helps out without a requirement for begging or sacrifice, the two are in constant communion and they understand each other better than anyone. We cannot choose our parents but we can choose whom we become friends with.

Resist the urge to disregard this concept on the basis of it being a delusional fallacy and contemplate what it would mean if he were our best friend? If we were going to believe in something wouldn't it be better to believe in something that serves us rather than something that requires something from us? If God were as almighty and powerful as religion implies, why would he have the wherewithal to ask us for what he needs? Think that he cannot attain anything he requires on his own? There is nothing we need to do, be or have to earn his love. So if God were our best friend wouldn't it imply that life has our back? That we are loved and supported no matter what we do and if we ever stray he will be waiting with arms open? Be open to the possibility that what we think we know may not serve us and that there is a new belief system we can put into place that can bring about change on a global scale. Life is on our side so let us ask questions that encourage change; put the universe to work, reflect what we intend to experience, request its love and support. Life loves us infinitely and wants us to awaken to our potential. Stop talking about how things are and start talking about how things could be.

2.6 What feeling stuck really infers

'You're not stuck. You're just committed to certain patterns of behaviour because they've helped you in the past. Now those behaviours have become more harmful than helpful. The reason why you can't move forward is because you keep applying an old formula to a new level in your life. Change the formula to get a different result.'

- Emily Maroutian

Feeling stuck is a state of being derived from the belief that we are powerless to change, that life is happening to us and we react to it. In other words we are at the mercy of a higher power and must pray that hopefully it will occasionally be kind to us. Feeling stuck can be an uncomfortable emotion that entails feelings of lethargy, apathy, depression, restlessness and frustration. However it is again simply another tool of the fear mind that keeps us apart from our true potential. It is important to understand that each moment presents a choice and that nothing is static. Change is an inevitable process of life that we must all go through as we grow and adapt to new circumstances; therefore, the feeling of being stuck must be illusory. Feeling stuck is usually sprung from a desire to experience something greater than our current reality but the fear of change restricts action.

When we constantly emanate a feeling of being stuck we create our experiences from that point of attraction and the universe simply reflects that state of being back to us in the form of experiences that produce more of that stuck feeling. In this state of confusion new ideas are not very tantalising, action is half-hearted, and we are more prone to depression. However if we believe life is on our side, we can see it as an opportunity to further refine what we desire and walk towards it. If we truly want things to change yet do not take the action required we will continue to remain feeling stuck. Too often people expect outside circumstances to change on their own yet perform the same actions that yield the same results.

For example, a woman who complains of encountering men who only use her for sex yet continues to sleep around is going to feel stuck. She may attribute that to her inability to meet men wanting to commit themselves to a long-term relationship but she is unaware that the dominant vibration she is offering attracts only men disinterested in long-term relationships or with her specifically. This may be attributed to an unconscious belief that power comes from using men before they use her, which fulfills her short-term need for power yet in actuality strengthens the discord between what she wants to experience and what she is experiencing now. She continues to perform casual sex to fill the void that becomes deeper until she pops and is forced to look within for what she desires. The first call of action she would need to take to break free from the feeling of being stuck would be to accept where she is. The woman needs to become aware that her thoughts and actions are inhibiting her from experiencing her true desire for love. Acceptance of where she is without judgment or condemnation brings about the possibility of change.

She would need to reformulate her definition of success so that she no longer sees casual sex as a form of power and that the love she craves is an intrinsic quality that must be cultivated within before she can experience it extrinsically. To ensure change extends into physical reality she must alter the habitual thought patterns producing the same actions so that she no longer feels compelled to sleep with men before they get to know her, which will shift her vibration from one of, 'use and abuse me,' to, 'I am worthy and expectant of love.' Anyone still in the woman's life who does not reflect back this change in vibration will either fade out or change what they offer her. She will become repulsed by the men she used to find attractive and find solace in the enjoyment of her own company, which in turn will become a very attractive quality for men who seek long-term partnership. With the inner change fulfilled her personal power will have heightened, she will no longer possess a void begging to be filled with the man closest to her, her point of attraction will no longer include men who use her, she will have more clarity about her true desires and, for the first time, she will come into alignment with her new man.

Change is not always an easy process but it is immensely rewarding. It takes courage to admit that the only person responsible for our emotions and state of affairs is our self. No matter how deep our pain, no matter who hurt us, no matter our age, we have the choice to create ourselves anew in every moment. Feeling stuck is nothing but a resistance to using our power to choose again. It is truly possible to move in the direction of our dreams and once we do we will have the benefit of hindsight. We will be able to look back on our life before the great change and recognise with true clarity how far off we were from embracing our potential. The process of change may seem to require much effort but when the process is enjoyed everyday brings something new that far outweighs a lifetime of subpar happiness, or even misery. We must fall in love with the process. Our desire to change must be so strong that the opportunity to counter it no longer poses temptation. We have the ability right now in this very moment to choose a life filled with the most unconditional love, joy, happiness, abundance, ease and flow. We can choose to share it with people who love and support us, or those who use us for their own interest. We can choose to work at a job that brings opportunities of growth, happiness and excitement or we can put our head down and continue talking about how change is risky. We can choose to eat foods that support a healthy immunity or continue to numb ourselves with commercial food. The choice is ours in every moment; what will you choose?

2.7 Taking responsibility for our emotions

'There is only one way to avoid criticism; do nothing, say nothing and be nothing.'

- Aristotle

When we take something personally we are reacting under the impression that we are not supported by life. The fear mind is hardwired for survival and happiness is a luxury. Our hereditary thinking habits train us to identify threats or things that are wrong in our experience so that we can live in safety. If our brain is locked into this habit of thinking we will forever be looking for ways we can be unhappy. Even when something great happens we will have an excuse for a way to feel down and turn it into a negative experience. If something occurs that threatens the image of the small self it is not taken lightly. Many arguments, wars and bans have been initiated over an inability to let things go. Rather than allow the experience to move through it gets caught in an old belief system, which the fear mind takes personally and uses as an excuse to hold us apart from our own wellbeing.

For example, a child in the playground is approached by a fellow playmate who laughs and calls him a homosexual. If the boy possesses no opinion or disposition about gays he would easily ignore the comment or walk away. However, if the boy was raised in a household that condemned gays or believed them to be inferior he may take the comment personally and react with rage. A belief system that triggers identification with the small self traps the comment. Without judgment the comment would go by unnoticed and no strong emotional response would be triggered, except for perhaps the derogatory tone behind the assumption. The benefit of not taking things personally is we release the need for others to please us. When we take our source of pleasure away from other people we have the freedom to create joy for ourselves in whichever way we please. This assists in taking the strain off relationships and provides us with the skills to create our own pleasure. Expectation for others to satisfy us is a shallow pool that only breeds disappointment and neediness.

Taking ownership of our own thoughts and emotions is a pivotal step on the way to inner transformation. All around us we see evidence of people living in fear that they are not good enough, that they are horrible people or the victims of horrible people, that happiness is a sparse commodity or that they need to *be* something to *get* something. A common misconception among people living in fear is that they will be happy once their desires manifest, but if life is a constant unfolding of desire they will never experience satisfaction. Once they get the job, the car, the money, the man, or the house they will then allow themselves to be happy. They say, 'once I move out of home, once people start treating me with respect, once he sees what I'm worth, once I get the girl, once I stop smoking, once the house is renovated then I can relax.' These types of excuses are examples of people outsourcing their power to external circumstance where happiness does not exist. Some are driven by a burning desire for success only to discover once they find it they are still miserable. Looking outside of ourselves for what we need is like trying to change the mirror instead of changing our outfit. Whether we train ourselves to look outside for joy or despair we are still giving our power away to reality and avoiding the responsibility of owning our emotions. Responsibility should not be misconstrued as a burden, it should be seen as the key to liberation. When we take responsibility we have the ability to experience joy regardless of what is going on and more clearly direct our attention where we want it to go. Ownership gives us freedom.

2.8 Aligning with our purpose

'Behind every problem is a question trying to be asked, behind every question there is an answer trying to be revealed, behind every answer there is an action trying to be taken and behind every action is a way of life trying to be born.'

– Michael Bernard Beckwith

Motivation is transient and not the most reliable source of action, but purpose allows us to execute our vision even on our off days. Without purpose there is no motivation. For many of us it is a fickle or fragmented concept that seems to evade us, always leaving us feeling unsatisfied, disempowered and wanting more. For others it seems to find them easily and effortlessly at a young age, always having something to guide them through life. If purpose has eluded us we could ask, 'why me?' and receive a million different answers that will not get us any closer to discovery. However, it is important to not confuse purpose with natural talent. While some may have the ability to naturally master a skill and, fortunately, the means to pursue it, purpose is given to the practice, not the other way around. The practice is the muse in which purpose is expressed; it is the medium through which we bridge the gap between the outer world and ourselves.

We all share the same purpose, which is to show up as our true authentic self. When we do not feel joy in what we do we feel we are without purpose. The empowered person uses this feeling as an opportunity to redefine their desires and discover what brings them joy, whereas the disempowered person holds other people accountable for the way things are. The empowered person asks empowering questions that stimulate creativity in the brain and clear the space for new ideas. The disempowered person says, 'why me? Why couldn't I have been born into a wealthy family? Why don't things ever work out for me?' They fawn on others who are living their dream yet secretly wish to remain the same to avoid the effort of change.

We will know we have found our purpose when our practice immerses us in the present moment. The feeling of joy is found when we release all contradictory thoughts of resistance triggered by memories and opinions of the fear mind and become one with the present moment. We have all experienced this feeling when we are blissfully lying on the beach, aimlessly painting, playing an instrument, picnicking in the park, swimming in the ocean or doing something that causes us to forget that we even need a purpose. In these moments we are completely absorbed in the now; oblivious to the train of negative momentum and completely attuned to our stream of wellbeing. When we are in this state of allowing the universe is more easily able to respond to the vibration of our desires, which is why we often have moments of revelation in the shower. If our state of being is predominately one of joy, happiness, peace and love we would be open to an entire world of ideas and opportunities we could never conceive of.

It all begins by discovering what we are meant to do. Every person on this planet without exception was born with an interest, talent, or ability that puts them of service to others. The way we perform service to the world is by living out our purpose and being in connection with our stream of wellbeing. We are of no use to anybody or ourselves if we are constantly disconnected from our true source, feeling uninspired and being unpleasant company. One person connected to their source has more power than a million who are not. When we are living our purpose our motivation to pursue our calling becomes so strong that it outweighs anything that counteracts it. For example, a professional athlete's burning desire for a fit body outweighs the desire to continue unhealthy eating habits. Anyone who is not in support of our vision or anyone who tries to convince us to pursue something more 'safe' or 'substantial' will fade out like white noise as our mind set will have shifted from 'why me?' to 'why not me?' When we open up to our stream of wellbeing and come into full alignment with our new and inspired vision of who we are, we will be supported by the universe in ways we could never imagine. We will experience new possibilities, new ways of thinking, new ideas and new ways of being that were previously invisible to us. In truth, the ideas and opportunities have always existed but when we become clear about what we want, embrace the new and intend to live a life of greatness our brain will be forced to look outside of its habitual ways of thinking for these new ideas.

Whether we believe it or not the universe is always responding to our point of attraction and will support us in whatever we decide to experience whether it brings pain or pleasure. The universe does not favour those who volunteer service for those in need over people who do not. It is an unbiased cosmos of energy that responds to all life that inhibits its shores for if everything is a derivative of God then everything is worthy of equal love. If volunteering to plant trees brings us pleasure then the universe responds to the vibration of joy we feel in the moment of planting, not to the idea that salvation is brought to good Samaritans. A woman immersed in playing piano is in complete harmony with her inner being and in doing so offering a service to others by allowing listeners to feel their emotions through the music. Discovering our purpose requires consistently asking empowering questions like:

- What is emerging in my life?
- How can I be of service?
- What are my natural talents and abilities?
- What is something I've always been interested in?
- What is the universe trying to express through me?
- How can I express my greatness?
- What is the next step I need to take?
- What is the vision for my life?

This is a contemplative process that requires openness and patience so that the mind does not hasten to provide incomplete answers that only temporarily fill the void of dissatisfaction. Allow thoughts to drift into awareness without judgment or attachment. The universe has the answer to every question we have about our lives and the more inspiring the questions, the more inspiring the answers. Counteracting grand ideas with arguments about what is 'realistic' limits our perception of what is possible and limits us to a small, reactionary life, whereas believing in the possibility of big ideas empowers us to think in ways that stimulate creativity and growth. Habits that stunt growth festers emotions of lethargy and apathy whereas habits that stimulate growth supports emotions of joy and fulfillment. Tuning into and strengthening thoughts of love is a skill that can be mastered and over time, depending on the intensity of intention, will become the only voice we listen to.

2.9 Changing the world by changing ourselves

'One of the most courageous decisions you will ever make is to finally let go of whatever is hurting your heart and soul.'

- Brigitte Nicole

Inner transformation is a personal process that is not limited to the self; it affects the whole world around us. Every time we choose to think a new thought we cause an affect that changes our reality including the people around us. We can turn on the media at any time of day and find an excuse to believe the world is in a terrible state but rather than dwell on feelings of hopelessness, fear, pity, rage, or sadness we can have an impact on the outer world through the power of our inner world. Too often we see kind, well meaning people believe they are victims to corporations who inflict global turmoil. We have created a world of division where the poor verse the rich; men verse women; white verse black and so on. One party enforces their illusion of superiority and the other party compensates by finding power in victimhood.

We give meat industries permission to farm millions of hectares of rainforests to raise the cattle that feeds our belief that red meat is the most substantial source of iron and protein. We give permission to major fashion retailers to exploit and underpay foreign workers so that the western world can decide what they *feel* like wearing. We give pharmaceutical companies the power to teach us pills are our savior yet we have more health related problems than ever before in history. Mining companies continue to destroy local communities and natural habitats to profit off unrenewable energy sources despite the availability of sustainable energy solutions.

In the book *Ishmael*, author Daniel Quinn explores the concept of a world of takers and givers. The Fertile Crescent is a large section of nutrient rich land in a region of the Middle East laden with farms and agricultural activity. With the discovery of fertile land, 'The Takers' were able to grow whatever food they wanted despite limitation of seasonality, whereas 'The Givers' lived in accordance with the seasons. The Givers were content with the variety nature provided them with whether that meant feast or famine. The Takers, however, were determined to survive and populate so they defied the natural rhythm of life by establishing agriculture. As such, horticulture was born, natural foraging was rendered barbaric, and farming became their new way of life. Cattle were fenced off in respective areas according to their uses, vegetables planted in rows, and poultry caged for the purpose of food production.

The Givers are what we currently refer to as native tribes, for example Native Americans, Peruvians, Amazonians and Indigenous Aboriginals to name a few. The population of these tribes has drastically dwindled and their way of life heavily compromised by The Takers who impose upon them their values of economic growth. They cultivated the ability to eat whatever they wanted, whenever they wanted and however much they wanted, which enabled their population to expand exponentially. But of course with more people comes more demand so agriculture expands, technology is created to support production, more energy is required, waste becomes an issue, pharmaceuticals are created to counter sickness created by poor diet, barter is replaced with currency, native tribes are pushed out of their homeland, food is in surplus, racial supremacy is created to enforce more 'forward' ways of thinking and humans take over the role of God.

Over time as our priorities shift from hunting and gathering to potential career prospects we have forgotten what it means to live. The purpose of life is not to be successful but to experience the joy of watching success unfold. This world we live in is polluted with contradictions; we criticise those who do not succeed and those who do, we reward the rich and tax them dearly, we extend aid to the poor and simultaneously deprive them of basic necessities. We can spend hours tirelessly pointing out every contradiction but that is not the point; we have the power in every moment to think a new thought that supports love and growth. While it serves us to understand how the world came to be, blame holds us apart from our vision of better. Knowledge is only synonymous with power when we can use the outcome of past decisions to create new ones. The actions of The Takers fulfilled their vision for population growth grew from an original, sponsoring thought of lack, and powerlessness. Takers expressed a desire to explore the role of power and decided they would not let the natural rhythm of nature limit their new and expanded idea of who they could be.

The crisis that currently exists is derived from the outcome of choosing to believe in separation from source. We are living out the reality of an illusion that brings pain, fear, and imbalance. We are living in a hell of our own making and the moment we give up the illusion of separation and return to source the sooner we can experience heaven on earth. Life is calling us to expand our idea of the self by opening up to love, peace and joy. The problem does not reside in the action of The Takers but in the sponsoring thought of fear, which still lingers to this day, though we are seeing evidence of this being challenged. If we are to change the outcome of the earth, we need to change the sponsoring thought from one of powerlessness and separation to love and support. In other words to transform the outer world, we must transform the inner world. That is the work we need to undertake.

It is important to keep in mind that life on planet earth is a mere concept. Our true nature has no form and in the realm of the formless there is no you and I, only unity. Life on earth is a platform for us to discover who we are by experiencing what we are not. The opportunity exists for us to restore wellbeing, but worst-case scenario; the end of the world is not really the end of the world. How can we die when we have no form? Life is but a game and we have all the tools we need to create the life we want. If we continue to live life the way we are we will continue suffer, so we have a choice; continue to think thoughts of fear or transform our inner world with love. We are the empowered people that have the courage to change. We are the ones that are crazy enough to believe that peace is possible, and it all starts within.

There is no need to take on the burdens of the world or feel we are responsible for other people's actions or emotions. The more time we spend flowing our attention to what is 'wrong' with the world or the people running it the more we prolong the suffering we are trying to change. Remember, where focus goes energy flows so if we want to change something on the outside we must take our attention off what is going on externally and center it on our vision of what could be. It is easy to fall into unhelpful, negative habits of thinking when exposed to a constant stream of negative media reporting but that does not mean we have to fall into victimhood and give our power away. While we may not be able to directly change the situation at hand at this moment in time we have the power to change the way we feel, which is much more powerful than focusing on current circumstance. It only takes one person connected to their stream of inner being to think of a solution to a big problem. We can be that person when we process the blocked emotions that impede our access to the stream of wellbeing and focus on a new vision with purpose. Let us envision a world that reflects an inner world of love, peace, joy and beauty.

2.10 Transforming blame and forgiveness

'Your actions reveal not what you want but what you choose.'

- Shane Parrish

A common way of palming off responsibility for our emotions is to hold someone else accountable. Employing another person as a scapegoat for our emotions is an easy way of dodging the discomfort that comes from hearing the truth that is emerging behind the pain. Undertaking transformation of the inner self is a process that requires intention, consistency, patience and persistence whereas blame allows us to bypass the process and continue activating negative habits. Pain is the inner self communicating with us that the thoughts and actions we are executing are not in alignment with love and require some fine tuning. Habit is an amazing tool we can use to our advantage to cultivate practices that stimulate joy, love and growth if used wisely. Smoking is an example of a detrimental habit that causes the body long-term distress. The habit that fulfills the emotional need for smoking outweighs the body's rejection of the poison.

Another example is a woman who hates her job and is unsatisfied with where she stands in life. She feels an intense desire to grow and experience something greater yet is unsure what action to take. One day she experiences an unpleasant event at work, which makes it unbearable for her to continue her employment. She attempts to outwardly reconcile the situation by reporting the incident yet experiences a lack of cooperation with management and decides that to protect her happiness she must leave. Life responded to her intense desire to expand by making her job, which previously felt safe and confortable, the exact opposite, providing her with the opportunity to move in the direction she wanted to go. The experience caused her to look inward and identify what habits of thought she was activating that kept her stuck and what new thoughts she could activate to bring about success and happiness. If she has no judgment about the experience she can use it as an opportunity to progress in her career but if it is taken personally she will face pain. She now faces the choice to blame the unpleasant event or use it to transform her inner world. While her reason for extreme negative emotion may be justified, continued blame stimulates suffering.

It is important to remember that life responded to her desire to expand, created a path of least resistance and found characters in her story that facilitated growth. While on a physical level she may blame the unpleasant event for having to change her life, in the realm of the invisible it assisted her in overcoming negative habits, awakening to her true potential and taking the action needed to reflect the change she wished to see. This realisation gave her permission to feel gratitude for the experience and cease using it as an excuse to feel consistent negative emotion. If she were to internalise the situation and take it personally, resentment would fester, which could compound into a trauma that then escalates into a state of being. In this case she will not have responded to life's call for expansion and will experience another situation of a similar nature until she changes the way she needs to. Blaming the event weakens her ability to see clearly, whereas owning the emotion gives her the strength to move on.

Using another example, a husband cheats on his wife of two children with a close friend. The wife whose best interest is in keeping together the family ignores the pain of the affair and attempts to mend the marriage with forgiveness. The husband, still unsatisfied with the marriage, secretly continues the affair until he is found out. The pain of betrayal and abandonment is so strong in the woman she eventually divorces him and assimilates the negative emotion into her new normal. In this case she does not own her emotion and therefore remains ignorant of the message that is trying to emerge through the pain. While the woman has every right to feel betrayed and can eternally blame him for breaking up their family, this thought does not serve her desire for love and happiness. If we explore her subconscious we may discover memories that support the opinion that men cannot be trusted.

If the emotion of betrayal is not fully processed it is internalised as a story and becomes a point of attraction that life responds to with like experiences. However, if she sees the experience as an opportunity to heal blocked emotions and redefine her vision she can create a new life that flourishes with love, creativity and joy. Eventually she will not use the husband as an excuse to hold herself apart from joy and she will commune with her inner being, the only relationship that matters. With hindsight she can feel gratitude for the infidelity revealing the ways she was limiting herself and inspire in herself and others the ability to transform the inner world. If the opportunity for growth is not ceased she will likely form an opinion about men that manifests in future relationships. We have the choice to think any thought we want, so why not choose joy over suffering? What have we got to lose by choosing to believe in the unconditional love and support life has for us?

It is important to be clear about the vision we are working towards. Our life vision should entice and inspire; it should make us want to leap out of bed in the morning. Whether we know the specific details of what we want or not, intend to live a life of greatness filled with the most love and joy ever experienced before. Life is but a dream and we have the ability to create it the way we want. The events that occur in the world are outcomes of stories we collectively agree upon. Stories are the fabric of our identity and help shape meaning in our lives but it is important to remember they are only suggestions. If the story is causing pain and misery, throw it out. We have the power right now to radically transform the world in any way we wish. Blame and criticism prolongs our story of suffering whereas love and purpose transform it.

Let us use the manifestation of what we do not want to create a vision for what we do want and consistently focus upon that new story. We all have access to the same stream of energy that gave Einstein the idea to create the light bulb and the Wright Brothers the idea to invent the first airplane. We have the choice to use that power to help us achieve our vision for a better future or continue the stream of negative momentum. Every person we come into contact with is a character in our play and only we have the ability to write the script. Finding pleasure in seeing those who hurt us be unhappy is not conducive to creating an environment of love and joy and will only keep us in victimhood. How can the world be full of love if it is kept from those that hurt us? When we see the beauty in the process of life we are more easily able to flow our love. We are shedding a light unto the darkness and when we see the perfection in all of life's creation we begin to be fed by life. There is nothing that is not worthy of our love for life is here to support us in all ways. With enough deliberate thinking we will be happy *because* of what is going on in our lives, not in *spite* of it.

2.11 Where our thoughts come from

'Most of us have two lives. The life we live and the unlived life within us. Between the two stand resistance.'

- Steven Pressfield

The exact words we use in our thoughts are nothing but interpretations of emotion. When we are in a negative mood we are more likely to think negative thoughts that reflect back and confirm the emotion. For example, intense sadness attracts thoughts that inspire more sadness with stories we have fabricated about the way we feel like, 'I'm not good enough,' 'this always happens to me,' 'what did I do to deserve this,' 'I should have handled it differently,' 'why does no one stand up for me,' etc. In reality life is not responding to the words we are using but the energy behind them. Thoughts make up part of the story of our identity so if we are wanting to change our state of being we must tell a different story, one where our thoughts uplift and inspire, not create more sadness. When we are in a state of being of joy and appreciation our mind automatically and with ease presents to us thoughts that match those emotions. Thoughts, emotions and words are all interconnected to our sense of identity so if we are wanting to make a change to our state of being the easiest way to initiate change is to ask, 'What kind of thoughts would I be thinking if I was living my dream life? How would it feel?'

An unhelpful albeit common suggestion for those experiencing chronic negative emotion is to find a therapist or trusted friend to talk about the problem with. Talking about an issue can help the person to accept ownership of their emotion but continuously talking about it activates negative energy and prolongs suffering. Consistently telling others how bad we feel and justifying it with stories is a bottomless pit that leads to despair and depression. That is not to say we should avoid seeking professional medical advice but if we want to grow from the pain of trauma it is helpful to feel the negative emotion and talk only about our vision for what is possible, rather than how bad we feel. In the thick of pain this can be a difficult task but if we do our best we cannot fail. It is entirely possible to change our lives for the better with the decision to ask for a different experience. We have a choice in every single moment to continue negative momentum or shift our attention in the other direction. If you are feeling pain and wanting to tell someone about it, do you have the intention of reconciling with it or pulling the other person into the drama?

Having a conversation with someone who intends, whether consciously or unconsciously, to bring others down to their level sounds like, 'So I have this thing going on that I really don't like and let me tell you all about it. It was awful, they were so mean, they're the reason I feel this way and can you believe what they did? The lack of support I have received is just horrendous. I would try to get better but now my dog has cancer, my father is ill, I don't have enough money, the government is corrupt and for some reason no one wants to listen to me. For every one thing that goes right in my life three things don't. Doesn't this just suck for me?' This type of conversation intends to rope the other person in and often leaves both parties feeling drained. They try to capitalise off other people's sympathy to compensate for their lack of personal power. Sometimes they can be very conniving and make us laugh at their story, leaving us wanting more but often these people feel alone and latch onto those who feel sympathy for them. This type of behaviour in people is often described as toxic.

A conversation with someone who intends to reconcile with their emotion sounds like, 'I'm really looking forward to what the future brings. Now that I've had this eye opening, clarifying experience I know that only I have the power to change my reality and I am actively taking steps to find my way home. Some days that looks like meditation and mindful eating, other days it looks like intense crying and spending the day in bed. I am aware that there is no such thing as a step backward, there is only what I choose to experience in the present moment. It's nice knowing there are people who can help me and I allow in support from all sources whether that be through therapy or going on daily walks. What will emerge from this pain is joy, clarity, peace and an understanding that I am adored by life and supported in every decision I make. I ask of you to remind me of this in moments where I feel consumed by the past or what is going on right now so that I can feel hope. I intend on using this experience to help me live a life of greatness and I look forward to becoming all that I can be.'

The difference between the two conversations is that one comes from a position of victimhood and needing to scrounge energy off others, while the other recognises the potential attempting to emerge through the pain. There is no one right way to process pain and we are all working to find ways to open ourselves up to our stream of wellbeing. For some that is through meditation and others alcoholism. Judge not the coping mechanism of another and instead remain centered in the awareness that we all have our own guidance system calling us home. We can help others by giving them the space to grow in their own time and becoming an example of what is possible. Rather than dogmatically enforcing our opinion onto others, even if it comes from the benevolence of wanting the best for them, understand that everyone is on their own journey and in the right place at the right time. It is impossible for anything to go wrong for in the eyes of our inner being we are perfect.

If we try to make sense of the way we feel by reliving past events we will most likely find evidence in everything we see. If we ask our brain to find memories that support our belief in lack we will inevitably receive an answer. The more we talk about something that upsets us the more intensified the negative emotion becomes and the more evidence we see of its manifestation. So how much should we vent about something before it begins to harm us? It depends on how intense or consistent the emotion is. If we are living out the manifestation of a constant stream of negative events and do not admit how we feel, nothing will change. Honesty enables us to accept where we are and get clear about where we want to go.

However, if we are aware of the negative experiences and constantly talk about them from a standpoint of unwillingness to change the more we prolong the suffering and cause it to manifest until it feels like a way of life. What we are really trying to understand by going over past events is not the specific incidents that caused the outcome but the emotion behind it. We try to understand 'what went wrong' by analysing our actions when really we should be looking at the emotion that inspired us to react the way we did. What belief caused the outcome? Did it come from insecurity? Or did it come from a fear of abandonment? If our state of being is anything other than love then change it. When we are encapsulated by love any negative experience will roll through our awareness with ease, we act with clarity and we become proactive not reactive.

2.12 Merging consistency and purpose

'Inspiration exists, but is has to find you working.'

- Pablo Picasso

Consistency is used to build new neural pathways that support the execution of habits that support growth. Purpose compounded with consistency motivates us to take the first step and follow through until the manifestation of a desired outcome. A person whose motivation to lose weight is derived from self-hatred will be able to take the first step in breaking a habit but without passion will struggle to follow through. A person whose motivation is sustained by the belief they deserve to feel good will be able to follow through and achieve their goal. Consistency is essential for building new habits and following through on our vision. When undergoing the process of inner transformation it is necessary to consistently choose a life of greatness with such intensity that it feels like we are saying it for the first time. In moments where we say, 'enough is enough,' or,' I can't take it anymore, things have got to change,' the power of intention sets off the current of momentum in a new direction. From there we choose new thoughts and build new habits that get us closer to where we want to be, which becomes easier to execute with repetition and passion.

When passion for the vision is amalgamated with enjoyment for the process we are able to consistently follow through on our actions. With these two in conjunction we evolve from 'having' to do something to 'wanting' to, allowing us to show up daily, look forward to our work, and face challenges with clarity. Passion that lacks a clear path leads to confusion and resentment as we cease to enjoy the action that is required for us to change. Likewise if we become attached to the outcome and forget to enjoy the process of enfoldment it is likely we will struggle to achieve our goals. When we take our attention off what is going on in the outside world and focus on the infinite world within results become complimentary. Life is an ever-changing rhythm that is always growing and renewing itself, and if we do not enjoy the process we will not enjoy anything. The satisfaction of achieving our dream will be short-lived and uninspiring until we decide to feel joy right now.

If negative motivation becomes our primary driver for action our mind may try to sabotage our efforts with old beliefs about the self. As the mind adjusts to new actions and ideas of the self it may occasionally throw a tantrum to communicate to us its dismay. This may come in the form of extreme negative emotion, headaches, the flu, or a general feeling of laziness. Using the 'no pain, no gain' method to push through the resistance will bring only short term profit but allowing it to pass through will speed up the process. We will inevitably face the temptation to revert back to what we perceive as safe but as the vision for greatness expands the desire will fade. Even a temporary relapse will not stand in our way. Inner transformation extends into the core of the self. It is about living from the potential of the unlimited self, not the bruised ego.

Progress can sometimes be high jacked by an emotional outburst or a mind attack as we learn to assimilate new habits. Extreme negative emotion may appear as a step backwards but what often surfaces after the storm passes is hope, inspiration and clarity. As we clear the emotions behind trauma and limiting beliefs the emotional outbursts become less frequent. Over time we are more easily able to execute new habits and fluidly move between emotions without attachment. With consistency our self-talk will evolve from internal bickering to deliberate, creative thinking. We will see no value in the story of the small self and if a mind attack encroaches we can sooth ourselves with a new story.

If a feeling of panic comes on try thinking thoughts like, 'all is well in my world, I am in the rhythm and flow of life, a feeling is just a thought and a thought can be changed, nothing has gone wrong, I am in the perfect place at the perfect time, I love and accept all that I am, the relief is just around the corner, I am relaxed and at ease, relaxed and at ease, I am supported by life no matter where I am, everything is working out for me, love emanates through my being and I accept it with open arms.' As we relax into our new state of being the story will become a way of life.

2.13 The comfort zone

'Fear doesn't shut you down; it wakes you up.'

- Veronica Roth

Short-term motivation encourages people to break through their comfort zones often when mental strength is premature and undeveloped, causing short-term gain and discouragement when they cannot break through the zone. The comfort zone is a concept created by fear that limits one from performing activities that put the self in perceived danger. For some people it can entail a practical fear of heights and for others a psychological fear that stimulates panic and anxiety. Experiences associated with any kind of pain usually imbue a desire to prevent the experience from reoccurring. Comfort zones are deemed a negative influence as they restrict our freedom to experience new things. Breaking them without addressing the sponsoring thought can counter the affect so that we become more ingrained in limitation.

Short-term motivational speeches encourage us to break free from the shackles of fear with words like, 'If you want to make your overwhelmingly big, daunting dreams come true you've got to sweat. You've got to struggle, work hard, put in the effort, have no fun, isolate yourself from others who bring you down (which, to some degree can be everyone), get up early, work when everyone is having fun so that one day when you attain all that you desire you won't have anyone to celebrate with but it will be worth it.' If the struggle to work for our dreams makes us resent the process, what is the point? If we do not teach ourselves to love then life will seem arduous and daunting. Short-term motivation inspires short-term change and if we want long-term effects we must undergo the process of inner transformation. The process of creation is deliberate, effortless, enjoyable and inspiring. It is natural, not forced, and allows room for rest, joy and contemplation.

Connecting to our inner being gives us the energy to connect with others and have compassion for those who tell us that what we want is not feasible. That is not to say we should agree with them but rather appreciate they are looking out for us in the way they know how, and gracefully choose to listen to our own guidance system.

With the influence of social media it is common to find people feeling pressured to do things they do not want to do. We are eluded into believing another person's highlight reel is their everyday life, sometimes making us feel inadequate and boring. During the time of transformation there may be a time of hermitage where we feel disinclined to engage in social activity that engages with old habits. We may wish to reject social invitations as we adjust to new ways of being. Activities that once seemed exciting may become boring as pleasure flourishes in activities that promote wellbeing. Soon self-obsession will graduate into an interest for others and we will want to participate in ways we can elevate global consciousness. Pushing our comfort zone to satisfy the perceived obligation that we should be doing more will not inspire us. Instead, let us relax in the knowingness that when the time is right we will become the recipient of an idea or opportunity that will inspire, delight and excite us. When it arises we will feel comfortable in accepting the invitation and there will be no need to push the comfort zone.

Eventually the threshold for what is possible will lift and our vision will expand. Rushing the process can be frightening and may cause us to revert back to old habits that masquerade comfort and safety, whereas patience for what is to come allows the mind to relax and continue to creatively envision new ways of being. The universe knows the perfect path, place and person for us to experience what we desire. When we open our self up to the stream of wellbeing there will be no need to push boundaries and cross comfort zones for we will experience true joy in saying yes to the opportunity that is presented to us. Life is a fun adventure and we agreed the day we set forth into this world to ride the rollercoaster.

Contemplation allows our soul to express its truth and the mind to express its fears. A sedentary life leads to stagnant ways of thinking and blinded busyness distracts us from the truth. We may feel an awkward push and pull as our vision causes us to grow and expand yet our fears will not shy from making them known. We are the light at the center that reconciles the two energies of yin and yang. Fear protects us from harmful circumstances and at times causes conflict with the energy of desire whose intention is to experience new things. Gentle contemplation allows for both energies to be heard without favouritism or judgment. The end goal is not to expel fear but to thank it for keeping us safe all these years and letting it know we are in control.

We can talk to the fear as if it were another person and say, 'thank you for always keeping me safe. You have done a marvelous job guiding me through life and telling me which opportunities I should say yes to. However, I can see you are stressed and I am here to let you off the hook. There is no need for you to hold so tightly anymore because I am here. I'm not trying to get rid of you, in fact I invite you to stay with me as I navigate through life and always whisper to me what you think is safe but I no longer need you in control. I'm sorry I haven't been there for you or listened in the past but I recognise your importance now and I promise to take more care.'

For a while we may notice no difference but with enough love and consistency the energy will naturally begin to shift. Initially we will first notice a difference in the way we feel; anxiety softens, depression fades, clarity emerges and joy creeps in. Mind attacks will occur less frequently as we disassociate with fear and with enough momentum we will experience an openness that may come as a pop in awareness or a sudden realisation that we are the observer of thought, not the participant. We will see that we are the ones influencing our thoughts and without any struggle or hard work our emotions will naturally respond to the new thoughts we are thinking. Daily walks are an excellent time to set our intentions and reaffirm our new story. Undisturbed time in nature allows for clarity of desire and thought. If we have the chance it is a good idea to go for a walk in nature, either solitary or with a trusted companion, and spend time contemplating our desires as if we are already living it.

What do you see? What do you feel? Where do you work? You could say things like, 'I am so happy and grateful now that I am living my dream life. When I wake up in the morning I am excited to see what opportunities the new day will bring, I am so grateful now that I have found my purpose and I am able to serve others and feel inspired. Life is a fun adventure and I am supported by life in every decision I make. New and exciting opportunities are knocking at my door. I always have enough money for the things I want and need for money is my best friend. I relax in the knowingness that there is no wrong decision, only what I feel inspired to choose in the moment and no matter what happens I am loved. I choose now to live a life of unbounded love and greatness. I am powerful beyond measure and I choose to express my power through service. I am grateful for all ideas that come my way. I am ready now to respond to my calling and live the best life I've ever imagined.' It is possible for us to experience the most love, joy, abundance and good we have ever conceived of. Behind us we have the energy that creates worlds, and with that kind of power anything is possible. There is no problem too big or too small for the universe to attend to and it responds with equal attentiveness to everybody.

2.14 An inner revolution

'The world doesn't need more successful people. The planet desperately needs more peacemakers, healers, restorers, story tellers and lovers of all kind.'

- Dalai Llama

Everything we have ever experienced up until now has been a series of choices we have made based on our understanding of how the world works. While we may not have a conscious choice of where we are born it is our choice what we do with our given circumstance. Stories give our lives meaning and purpose; they cause expansion and growth into new and exciting ways of being. Life is about expanding our sense of self and becoming one with consciousness. Culture is just another word for story that explains who we are, how we act and where we came from. The battles we have encountered, the land we have claimed, the countries we have formed, the races we have segregated and the political systems in power all form a collective identity that reflects who we think we are. We talk about the past, write textbooks about it, erect statues, hold memorials and activate the energy of these stories sometimes with the same propensity as if it were happening in the present moment. Let us not use our past to predict our future. Let us use memories to help us envision a future that includes peace and unity.

The pain we enforce on others for the sake of upholding traditions that no longer serve us is a demonstration of refusing to grow and expand into new ways of being. Even countries are nothing but a mere concept. A rebirthing takes place when we are finally able to look at our creation and assess whether it brings us closer to our inner being or further away. The choice may emerge out of an accumulation of pain or recognition that things simply could be better. Resistance to limiting circumstances initiates revolutions and a demand for higher standards of living, often causing protest, activism, crime, abolition of law, etc. The revolution gains momentum when more people protest against the pain and move towards the vision for a better future. In other words, the pain pushes until the vision pulls. Revolutions occur inwardly when pain becomes so significant the thought of prolongation conspires feelings of intense revulsion colloquially described as being, 'fed up' and typically ensues extreme retaliation. A call to action is mustered and the person evolves from a state of idleness to a state of action.

Violence is typically found in symbiosis with revolutions due to the intensity of passion fuelling the cause. Throughout the entire history of civilisation we can find evidence of misuse of power. The first agitation for women's rights dates back to 1848 in the United States where a group of women gathered to discuss the lack of equality between males and females, thereby birthing the fight for women's suffrage. Evidence of the imbalance of power well predated the movement but for the first time women decided to resist the assumption that they should be afforded less rights than men due to an assumption of weakness. Since the meeting more women have joined the reformation of women's rights by challenging assumptions, entering workplaces deemed for men, demanding a right to vote, restoring power over their body and more. The revolution was initiated by resistance to an outdated belief and with recruitment of like-minded thinkers caused a response that initiated the restoration of power between men and women.

A revolution combats the idea that power should belong to one group of people. The abolition of slavery was passed around the beginning of the nineteenth century in response to extreme resistance to the idea that a person can be treated as a mechanical possession of the government. Slavery still exists to this today in illegal forms as it responds to the demand for cheap labour, but as our species evolves and our priority shifts from greed to abundance, our vision expands into love. The agitation of black power rejected the idea of a minority and pushed for the need to be seen as equal. All revolutions are born from a resistance of misuse or imbalance of power. People do not fight against leadership; they fight against unfair distribution of power and for the right to be heard. If we study the process of revolution we are better able to understand how change unfolds in the mind.

Using the example of women's suffrage again, we will see that at some point an idea was formed that women were somehow inferior to men. In response to the belief, women were refused the same rights as men, therefore establishing an unequal distribution of power between sexes. Frustrations arose when the lack of power intensified and woman were unable to express opinions, undertake certain jobs, wear certain clothes, have one's own name printed on a passport, work while pregnant, and be treated with less respect than men. The imposed limitations caused pain and conceptualised a revolution that gathered members of the subjugated party to express resistance against the belief that women were weak, therefore pushing for a fair and equal distribution of power. Humanity was forced to evolve in its way of thinking and consider what new belief would reflect equality. The momentum of the reformation accelerated to allow for many changes and now has the support of many people, including members of the opposite sex, and continues to accelerate in momentum.

2.15 Belief and resistance

'Your task is not to seek for love, but merely to seek and find all the barriers within yourself that you have built against it.'

- Rumi

We can use the process of a revolution to better understand how change is initiated in the inner world. Once an idea becomes a belief a self-fulfilling prophecy is formed, meaning the belief upholds the action, and the action affirms the outcome. If we postulate that life is unfair we will take action in support of this, which produces outcomes that are unfair, thus reaffirming the belief. When belief and action are in alignment we create a state of being that is reciprocated with circumstances that are in harmony with the vision.

The first sign of evidence to suggest the beginning of a revolution is resistance to the current standard of living. This is usually shown through a bold statement of action simulating a crux in the original story. For example, it could be a declaration of war upon another country or a black woman refusing to give up her seat for a white woman. The action signifies defiance of the story and an expectation that things must change to reflect a more equal distribution of power. Feminists do not cry for the rule of women, the same as African Americans do not wish for racial dominance; they demand equal respect. Successful revolutions are persistent, adamant, open-minded and convincing. They convince the opposing party that their proposed new beliefs are the newest, expanded expression of consciousness. To successfully follow through with the resistance we must address the sponsoring fear.

If we believe we are at the mercy of a higher power this manifests into reality where one party assumes the role of God and the other the victim or worshipper until rebellion shifts the balance of power. When the outcome of an action causes pain it is a sign that a shift in thinking needs to occur, which is usually stimulated by a radical change of action. For example, Rosa Parks was deemed 'the first lady of the civil rights movement' by the United States Congress for refusing to give up her seat for a white woman, thus initiating a large-scale boycott. The intention behind the action challenged the belief in white supremacy and called for a reevaluation in thinking patterns. Our natural instinct to initiate change is to act in a way that draws attention to the point of pain and request a change in belief. A movement towards an improved way of being is achieved quickly and easily when the outcome of the new belief outweighs the desire to revert back to old habits. The balance for racial equality has taken some time to integrate, as it requires supremacy to be thwarted by unity. To ensure the successful acquisition of equality, the pleasure the fear mind takes from the illusion of power must be shattered and replaced with love, which to those who are deeply imbued with fear can be hard to conceptualise.

For example, a person wishing to quit smoking without addressing the underlying need for cigarettes may prove futile. He can question his need to smoke by asking, 'what need am I fulfilling?' 'What am I hiding behind the smokescreen?' 'What beliefs would need to be changed to eradicate my need to smoke?' The same questions can be asked in regards to any aspect of life. Using the example of women's suffrage we can ask, 'what need is being met when we assume the weakness of women?' 'Is it possible women can offer a strength men do not possess?' 'How can we distribute power in a way that serves all?' 'What message is trying to emerge in the movement?' The solitary act of changing action is excellent for initiating a change in momentum but long-term success requires consistent questioning of beliefs and motives.

It is as Rumi says, 'maybe you are searching among the branches, for what only appears in the roots.' It is not enough to rely on change to arrive through action alone, we must address the core belief that causes the outcomes we resist. When this is done change occurs quickly. People who successfully lead revolutions have been pushed by pain to envision a new way of being. We can reflect the process of revolution in our internal world by becoming so unrelentingly convinced by our vision that nothing can dissuade us from achieving it. People in support of our idea will naturally gravitate towards us and offer their services whereas those who oppose will see evidence of the manifestation and be convinced of a better way of living.

PART THREE

Transformation Of The Cosmos

'Each day of your life you are sowing seeds that one day you must harvest. When you have come to truly understand this, you will take your satisfaction from your work and never from your harvest. For the sowing of the seed is all any of us does in this life.'

-Uell Stanley Anderson

3.1 Falling in love with the process

'The only way to make sense out of change is to plunge into it, move with it, and join the dance.'

- Alan Watts

The process of inner transformation is quite spectacular in that it calls into question everything we think we know about our place in the world. Crisis calls for us to look inwards for answers to the most pressing questions about the nature of existence so that we can move forward with clarity and purpose. We did not enter into this world of duality having completely forgotten who we are; we came here to be creators by putting into practice all that we are. We embody our true self when we are joyously absorbed in the present moment and forget all contradictory thoughts of resistance that hold us apart from our vision. If we grant ourselves happiness only when we have arrived at a desired destination we will have missed the point and will likely find it more difficult to maintain the motivation needed to complete a task. Yet if we learn to find enjoyment in the act of doing something for the sake of it while simultaneously being guided by a goal we will find it much easier to continue doing the work needed, so much so that it is no longer considered work. Musicians do not consider showing up everyday to play their craft as 'practice', they do it out of sheer enjoyment regardless of whether they are successful or not. We will know we are on the right path when it becomes possible to show up daily for our work without finding it a burden.

Inner transformation realigns our connection with source. It feels like coming home because we finally look beyond what we see and into the heart of truth. When we use our mind to search for answers and grasp an intellectual understanding of what is happening we limit potential because our mind is nothing more than a collection of opinions based on past events. Dreaming big encourages our mind to expand in ways that allows source to provide us with new ideas we previously could never conceive of. Author Grant Cardone discusses a concept that expands the imagination in his book *The Ten Times Rule: The Only Difference between Success and Failure*, in which the reader is encouraged to take an idea and times it by ten. If it is our goal to acquire ten clients by the end of the year multiply it by ten to make 100. This encourages us to think big and consider new ways of being that the fear mind could never conceive as possible so that even if we only end up with only 20 clients that is still double the amount we originally planned to acquire. We will have more success finding inspiring ideas by feeling our way there rather than referring to past experiences that determine what is possible. Let us expand our concept of what is possible, believe in a life of greatness, learn from those who have achieved it and demand more from life. If you find yourself feeling stuck and unable to think clearly remember to ask empowering questions:

- How can I achieve my vision?
- What tools do I already have to help me get there?
- What resources do I already have?
- Who do I need to become to achieve my vision?
- How can I embody the woman/man I wish to be?
- What does she/he do differently than what I have been doing?
- How does she/he approach a challenge?

Awakening feels like letting it all go and letting it all in at the same time. True awakening allows us to embrace all experiences without judgment because we become aware that life loves us unconditionally and is here to serve us. We understand that the world is nothing more than a reflection of our thoughts and victimhood is a tool of the fear mind used to keep us small. When this becomes our state of being we see every moment as a gift and release attachment to our emotions. This also makes it easier for us to deliberately create the life of our dreams as we release our attachment to permanence. We can hold the idea of a potential reality and have fun working towards it but when we are enjoying the process and understand that joy comes from presence we immediately come into connection with that new and expanded version of reality. When this occurs we do not even need the idea to come to fruition, though it will, because we will already be experiencing joy.

Awakening to our true self causes us to love who we become in the process of change and thank the trauma or crisis that caused us to expand. Life truly is here to support us and there is no need to die in order to experience heaven on earth. The moment we choose to end our own suffering by prioritising the way we feel over our circumstances we will have acquired a very useful tool that can be used maintain a clear vision. We will emanate an undeniable presence that others will either fear or be magnetised by. This presence gives us the ability to remain empowered when the world is doused in fear and acquire clarity in the face of confusion. Those stuck in the grips of the fear mind may try to bring us down to their level but we will be discerning of these characters and remain in the heart of truth. If someone attempts to bring us down we will know they are acting from their own personal hell that has nothing to do with us. Stimulating their behaviour with a negative emotional reaction validates their desire to matter whereas acknowledging their personal suffering gives them the opportunity to heal. Through our own connection with source we can teach others how to ask for our needs to be met without throwing an adult tantrum.

Releasing attachment to our external reality immediately flows less energy to people and circumstances that drain us and onto the endless stream of wellbeing that is always flowing to us. Life is not about making do with what we have been given and identifying as a victim, it is about seeing the potential trying to emerge in every experience. Heaven is when we are in harmony with our greater vision and enjoy the experience of watching it unfold before it even arrives. It is possible to eagerly await our manifestation with anticipation and excitement while showing up to do the work. Buddhist monks have been known to thank God in advance for their wish as if it were already here to speed up the process of manifestation. Our desires are a product of thinking big, believing in the beneficence of the universe and consistently showing up. When we release our attachment to how things should be on the outside we free up space in our mind for envisioning new possibilities. We cannot experience new opportunities if our mind is filled with past thoughts that only recreate past traumas.

Upon death we lose attachment to our identity because in the realm of the invisible it is meaningless. Everything we once held as important has no impact and we return once again to the home of our inner being where there is no resistance to our true nature. True awakening is becoming aware that there is no such thing, for how can we awaken to that which we already are? While we may label an experience as unpleasant our soul loves it for everything is born of love and is always guiding us back to that. When we realise this, life becomes more enjoyable as struggle is replaced with anticipation and hard work is relinquished with passion. Life does not require anything of us; there are no expectations, not even preferences, it is up to us what we choose to experience so let us not take it seriously. When we realise the truth about our existence it is easier to release trauma because we understand that what we put our attention on grows and becomes more important. Once we remove our identity from the situation and redirect our thoughts during a relapse we will over time feel lighter and more joyous.

If we can shift our priority from things that inflate the fear mind like making money or accumulating power to feeling unconditional joy and love we will likely find our inner world transformed in a way that satisfies and inspires us. It has been said before that when we arrive at the gates of heaven we will not be judged on how many things we have accumulated or what people think of us, but of what we learnt and how much we enjoyed it. Imagine if the whole world shifted priority from greed to abundance; exploitation would cease, pollution would be better managed, people would be kinder to themselves and each other, and conflict resolution would prevent major unrest. We shift to a fulfilling life when we choose love over drama. The rumours spread about us, the people we were invested in, and the stories we wanted to play out all take a back seat when love becomes the driver. It requires persistence but eventually it will become our new state of being from which every action will be derived. We are fooled into thinking that the more things we accumulate the happier we will be as it is deeply ingrained in our subconscious that greed is good. Abundance is our natural birthright that flows to us with ease once we command it into our experience yet greed and frugality are born of lack. We are only needy when our needs are unmet, so if we can fulfill our need to feel loved and supported by showing up for ourselves we attract experiences that support abundance.

3.2 Allowing the presence of emptiness

'If one advances confidently in the direction of his dreams, and endeavors to the live the life which he has imagined, he will meet with a success unexpected in common hours.'

- Henry David Thoreau

When we feel hungry we eat, when we lose breath we inhale and when we are tired we sleep. Naturally when we feel emptiness we fill the void with something that will bring us back into balance. When we approach the near end of our inner journey we may feel a slight emptiness as we let go of all the things that do not serve us. It is an unusual feeling, as we are no longer distracted by feelings of hurt, betrayal or sadness but are not yet living our new manifestation in its full form. We will begin to see evidence of the shift being made through the way we feel and our interaction with others. It is almost like reminiscing as we look back on where we started and see how far we have come. It is important to occasionally look back and take stock of our progress so that in times when we may feel like nothing has changed we can see more has changed than we think. As our demeanor morphs into kindness and love we will notice these qualities reflected back to us by people we interact with. When we meet our own needs and not expect others to do it for us they are more willing to express their love. When we no longer expect people to act a certain way and allow them the freedom to be themselves in our presence they are much more likely to treat us with kindness. The ones who do not find their purpose with us will leave and those that do will stay, but this time it will be to the benefit of both parties, not just one.

We will begin to see in others the business of their mind as they react to drama, participate in negative gossip, and find ways to fill the gaping hole of spiritual starvation. Have compassion for these people for they are doing the best they can with what they know, just as we once did. In many cases when one experiences an emotional imbalance they rely on external stimulus such as relationships, drugs, drama, shopping or other addictions to reestablish equilibrium, only to find that the temporary solution to lack can only be fed, never satisfied. Addictions form when we are unaware how to meet our own needs and must manifest satisfaction through the illusion of the physical world. Addiction can only exist in the presence of fear, usually having to do with the belief that life is not supportive and we must use something outside of us as a crutch. Once the person reconciles with their belief that they are separate from source they are able to take the steps towards inner fulfillment and the need for the external stimulus naturally dissipates. For those of us who are taught that happiness is found in the acquisition of material possessions it can be confronting when we realise it is actually the source of misery. There is only so much we can acquire before we realise we are buying our way into darkness. Money is a tool that enhances our experience on earth and comes to those who choose to live their purpose. In the book *100 Things,* author Sebastian Terry recounts his experience of ticking off items from his bucket list. Terry remarked that as soon as he made it his intention to tick off an item the exact resources he needed to complete it came to his aid. When we make it our intention to live our dream and feel the excitement of that becoming true the universe conspires and presents to us the perfect circumstance for it to manifest.

At times we may stir drama or even label looking within as boring but this is a smoke screen created by the fear mind that keeps us from feeling pain. It is afraid that if we expose the beliefs we doggedly hang onto, hell will be raised, because that is exactly what will happen. The mind will be forced to meet itself and the creation of its own hell if it cannot release attachment to identity. The best way to think of the fear mind of is as a tick. It buries into our skin and hides away undetected for quite some time before our body begins to reject it. We feel an itch and quickly become aware of the insect that drains our blood and leaks poison into our system. The poison is the lies and limiting beliefs that convince us we need the tick in order to survive yet eventually the body throws a tantrum and we must remove the foreign insect. The longer we leave the parasite the harder it is to remove but the body comes to our aid and literally rejects it. When this occurs we feel an incredible lightness, like we are in our right mind and we can laugh again. We look at the swollen tick and realise we are not it, that we were infected with an illness that distorted our clarity and we can now squish it.

Removing the beliefs that provide the illusory experience of struggle enables us to interact with others in a way that enlightens and inspires. We will be so full to the brim with pure positive energy that we will rarely feel drained from another and we will delight in others benefiting from our presence. Many people strive to become 'somebody' so that they are worthy of love and attention but the true delight is in becoming no one. When we approach life with equanimity we are able to fluidly adapt between circumstances as life asks us to change. It is also easier to remain in the heart of truth during stressful circumstances or when those around us are involved in drama. When we are clear in the vibration we are offering we will know when to act, when to rest, when to leave and how to respond. The presence of emptiness expands the more we reconcile with past traumas and process blocked emotions, which may give us the impulse to fill up with old habits but this will eventually subside the more our vision pulls us. Allow the space to grow so that we can be energised by thoughts and emotions that inspire greatness. Filling it with junk including drama, tantrums or made up emotions will only hinder us from growth so let us be aware when our mind is playing tricks.

Enjoy the solitude that comes from raising standards and give yourself permission to dream up the biggest, most bold, amazing life to fill it with. In moments of quietude talk to consciousness and request its help so that we can walk towards our vision with ease. Choosing to change takes enormous courage but eventually we discover that it is easier than we perceive. When we return to our life we will have a newfound energy that people will find infectious and inspiring. Those who hurt us or were hurt by us will see the change as we will no longer be operating from the fear mind that judges, condemns and holds grudges. We will see why we were hurt and no longer hold anyone accountable for the way we feel and thereby attract new experiences that reflect the expanded version of who we are. First come the new goals and then the friends who reflect them. When we are in the rather awkward stage where we have outgrown our old skin and have not yet met our new self we may experience a range of emotions including joy, inspiration, lethargy, confusion, nostalgia, frustration and sadness. Despite the doubts we may face eventually with enough persistence and conviction the space will be filled with the vibrant colours of love and inspiration.

3.3 The self as an illusion

'One should not excessively seek partners or friends, one should seek to know and be oneself. As you begin to awaken to the Truth, you start noticing how well life flows by itself and how well you are cared for. Life supports the physical, emotional, mental and spiritual needs of the one who is open to self-discovery. Trust opens your eyes to the recognition of this. Surrender allows you to merge in your own eternal being.'

- Mooji

Death is only a release from the story of the individual self and a return to collective spirit. We no longer identify as whoever we say we are, and everything we thought we possessed is relinquished back into the nothingness from where it came. For many of us this occurs at the time of death but for some it occurs during our time on earth as we consciously decide to dispose of the idea of separation. This form of awakening occurs when we are open to expanding our sense of self and choose to embody heaven on earth. When our expectation is replaced with appreciation our attachment to the self weakens and we are left with pure spirit. The illusions are seen for what they are and love becomes the driving force behind all our actions. That is not to say that when we are asked for our name we say, 'I am unidentifiable, a physical interpretation of invisible force from which all of creation is born.' No, we state our name and live our lives as normal but with the knowledge we are formless spirit having a physical experience. This is called death of the ego, or enlightenment, or the return to source.

What many people lack is an understanding of the basic laws of nature we can use to help guide us in making decisions and manifesting our vision so that we open ourselves to more joy and abundance. If we lived in the knowledge that life supports us and is always guiding us we would expect positive outcomes regardless of current circumstance. Negative experiences would never escalate into trauma or a prolonged negative emotional state because we will know that life is temporary and the actions of others never have anything to do with us unless we make it so. People who hurt us can still be held accountable for their actions but we free ourselves from a lifetime of inner turmoil when we release our attachment to reality and cultivate inner peace.

People in their twenties are commonly faced with a myriad of stressful situations including career change, breakups, financial pressure, internal conflict, moving out, and are an age group highly susceptible to anxiety and depression. A general belief held by older generations and imbued onto the youth is that life cannot be trusted and it is up to the individual to 'effort' their way to success through quality education, long hours and finding pride in struggle. Pain in gain is a misunderstood concept that implies a person can only attain what they seek through suffering and that true joy is only permitted once the goal is fulfilled, yet it begs the question; what is the point in attaining a goal if the process is not enjoyed? Once the desire manifests the feeling of satisfaction is short-lived and the whole process of creation is dreaded. Life is not an eternal struggle that seldom rewards; it is meant to be delighted over and experienced at its greatest. We do not have to live by the same beliefs we were taught by our elders if they do not serve us. While they have taught us the value of consistency and perseverance we have the power to choose beliefs that support fun, ease, love and growth. These beliefs determine our experience so it may be worth contemplating what supports our experience and what hinders it.

Contemplation is a gentle practice that creates space for emotions to arise freely without judgment. What contemplation reveals to us is the eternal nature of being and the untouchable spirit that resides behind the costume of identity. Who we are is not the collection of thoughts, opinions and beliefs we have conjured about our self; we are the formless spirit we long to be in connection with. The more we navigate life and solve problems using our mind the more distant we feel from our true nature but if we use intuition and faith as our compass we will be guided home. There is no need to talk about the past and activate the energy of painful memories; there is only the need to stand in the deliciousness of the present moment with a firm knowingness that all is well even when it seems otherwise. Our soul has no preference for anything, it loves every choice we make and every experience we choose for everything is ultimately a manifestation of love. The less we rely on the tools of the fear mind to solve problems the more life will unfold and prove its magnificence. It is impossible for us to be anything other than our true nature so let us throw away all limitations and make space for love to show up.

The idea that happiness lays in the future attainment of a goal is an illusion and will constantly leave us in a state of frustration and dissatisfaction. Giving up our potential for joy to something outside of our self invites fear and implies we do not trust that our needs will be met creating feelings of anxiety and tension, as we must rely on an external circumstance to be a certain way to ensure our emotional wellbeing. Obsession is born and then we must find a way we can keep that external source of safety alive so we can enjoy the illusion of security. This may work for a while but relying on anything other than our inner being for love and support creates the perfect breeding ground for depression and anxiety. When change occurs it is extremely painful for the fear mind, as the continuity required in keeping our identity alive is suddenly no longer able to support us and we are thrown into inner turmoil. Sometimes this is done on purpose by life to bring awareness to our attachment so we can undergo the journey of inner transformation.

Anxiety is a set of thought patterns responding to bodily sensations. Allowing the sensation of panic to roll through our body provides space for it to move freely and without judgment. The habitual thoughts associated with panic will wish to make themselves known but if we avoid associating with it and see it as just a bodily sensation we will in time lose the need to identify with it. Our initial reaction will be to judge or escape the sensation but relief comes from the knowingness that our eternal source of love dwells within. We have everything we need right now in this moment to feel the most bliss, love, joy and peace we have ever experienced. If we can train our mind to acknowledge that an external source of happiness is illusory we may initially feel resistance but this will eventually subside the more we tune into our heart. It may feel like our world turning upside down but it is nothing more than the pain of releasing attachment. Allow emptiness to emerge so that we may connect with our inner sense of peace. The more we do this the stronger our sense of connection will be and the easier it will be to find peace not from another but within. When we elect thoughts that come from a place of love we will look for and experience just that; love.

3.4 Setting up the experience

'Leap and the net will appear.'

- John Burroughs

An excellent tool we can use to set up a physical experience before it occurs is setting intentions. When we make a statement about the emotions we intend to feel before an experience unfolds we are likely to feel them. This tool can be used to enhance any social interaction, business venture, or other ordinary daily experience. The more we focus on the emotion we wish to feel behind an experience rather than a specific outcome the easier it is to direct our thoughts in that direction. For example a shift worker can set up their day how they choose by possibly saying to themselves, 'today is going to be an amazing day. I am going to encounter many wonderful customers and enjoy every minute. The time is going to fly by and I'm going to leave my shift feeling like it only just started. My managers will be impressed with my performance and I will be working with my favourite people.' This directs thought in the direction of joy and leaves space to have desires met in a way that may pleasantly surprise us. A person who may wish to experience more enjoyment at work may begin with thoughts like, 'I intend to feel successful in my work. I intend to love every minute of my job and feel gratitude for the exciting opportunities that come my way. My job is fun, rewarding and well paying.' This paves the way for more specific desires to be met once the overall feeling of joy has been achieved.

Success is achieving the state of happiness before the desire is made physical. When we get to this state momentum accelerates in the desired direction and any hard work that is required in the process of manifestation is perceived not as painful, but as a rewarding challenge that brings about immense satisfaction. Success is a product of unconditional love as it assumes the support of the universe. One who wishes to experience romance seeks the fulfillment of the need to be loved and supported by another. The need is immediately met when we can experience the true emotion behind the desire before it is met, which then brings us into alignment with the potential mate. The ultimate feeling behind any desire is joy and when joy becomes our predominate experience we can manifest desires with ease and clarity. Focus on the feeling behind the desire and amplify it with attention. If you have everything you need right now to be happy, why should you wait for your desire to be made manifest to feel great now? Centre your attention on the feeling of success and ask what it means for you. How do you hold yourself? How do you treat others? What thoughts do you think? Chronic scattered thoughts create a scattered reality but thoughts that intend joy bring about joy. Through awareness we attain clarity and through intention we manifest desires. We are in actuality setting intentions all the time with every thought but when we consciously curate thoughts about a subject then we can consciously create our reality.

A Course in Miracles states that sickness is a choice made out of the misconception that it is strength and that, 'Healing is accomplished the instant the sufferer no longer sees any value in pain. Who would choose suffering unless he thought it brought him something, and something of value to him? He must think it is a small price to pay for something of greater worth.' The only entity that benefits from the story of being small is the fear mind. Cut through the noise of fear with thoughts that bring about love and clarity.

3.5 The illusion of separation

'What others do to you is their karma, how you react is yours.'

– Wayne Dyer

There appears to be many problems in the world all that require our attention. There are many surface reasons why we hold ourselves apart from happiness but at the core of everything is the illusion that we are separate from source. It implies that every thought and action is isolated, that we are our minds and there is a beginning and end. Some studies in psychedelics reveal participants who ingested a hallucinogenic experienced the illusion of the self and an interconnectedness of all living creatures. If we are nothing but our minds then what appears to be true is the idea that every man is for himself, we are unsupported by life and we must apply effort to create the life we desire in this hellish realm from which we have been banished. We are abandoned, without power and without purpose. The idea of separation and a vengeful God is a misconception that causes much suffering from chronic illnesses to suffering in relationships and more. The only way we remedy this ailment in thinking is to understand that all beliefs are an illusion and we have the ability to believe what we choose. Every person has the freewill to think as they wish, so why not think we are loved and supported?

We live in a world where we have caused ourselves to forget that we are incredible entities living out potential in physical form. Doubt and curiosity are excellent tools of the empowered mind that assist in the employment of beliefs that enhance the sensation of love and weaken the argument for limitation. When we question the validity of our arguments we weaken the emotional intensity of our beliefs and create space for new potential. True liberation occurs when we realise we do not have to continue thinking the same thoughts if they do not serve us.

The only thing holding us back from a life of greatness is our thoughts about it. Once our image of our new potential self expands it requires us to think differently. We cannot attain something new by acting out the old. A shift in awareness occurs when we finally recognise that the perceived 'problems' of the world demanding our attention are born from the idea of punishment and retribution. Contemplating the interconnectedness of all living things brings us closer to the awareness that we are all one. The only thing that differentiates us from another is the vibration of molecules; at the core we are all made of atoms vibrating at different frequencies.

When a negative experience evolves into trauma we are told by others to forget the experience and go on with life but how can we achieve that when we have no power where our mind goes? And if during the day we somehow succeed in undoing the mental attachment to the trauma, it is likely we may relive it in our dreams and awake with the same emotional intensity as when it happened. Why does this occur? Why is it almost impossible to forget a negative experience? Perhaps it is a byproduct of separation. It is easy for our awareness to drift back to the event in the past, relive it, imagine what we would do differently, wish with all our hearts it had not happened, and even find ways to blame ourselves. We punish ourselves by reliving it over and over again without meaning to, as if hoping to finally understand what happened and how to prevent it from occurring again. The fastest though not the easiest way of healing trauma is to disassociate with the personification of pain. Who is the one that is traumatised? The pure spirit that we are born of remains in the heart of truth, untainted and unaffected by life's drama so that only leaves the fear mind.

Part of the healing process for trauma occurs when the fear mind continuously relives the event in attempt to form a narrative and clarify what happened so we can attach meaning to it. When we face trauma we are told many times to forget the past but what is not understood is that for many people this is a strongly resisted habit that cannot be helped. Time itself does not heal all wounds, we must treat the issue with love so it does not fester and take on the illusion of a monster. Acceptance of the way we feel is the easiest way to pass through the web of negative emotion without creating an identity that prolongs the pain and manifests in other areas of our life. Trauma is a strong emotional reaction to the feeling of abandonment and assumes disconnection from source. In this sense it is a gift from God that serves to indicate that what we think about our self is not in harmony with what our inner being thinks about us and with a strong intention can be used as an opportunity to allow in more love. If our inner being were a limitless supply of unconditional love and peace it would be impossible for that part of us to feel pain, rejection, guilt or shame.

If anxiety, depression, obsession, phobias, chronic illnesses and trauma can be passed down through generations how far into the past do we look until we find the sponsoring thought? What if the trauma we experience in our own lifetime is simply a manifestation of the collective fear felt by others? Understanding the emotion behind the cause compelling undesired habits may help guide us towards the sponsoring thought causing the illusion of separation from source. Author Mark Wolynn notes a scientific study in his book *It Didn't Start With You* that people whose parents suffered from post traumatic stress disorder (PTSD) were more likely to express similar symptoms of depression and anxiety whether they were aware of the past trauma or not. He touches on a patient who experienced extreme depression without any seeming reason and whose desired method of suicide was incineration. It was later revealed that her Grandmother's entire family was incinerated in the holocaust, which instigated extreme feelings of loss, guilt and sadness that were never mentioned by the grandmother. Untreated trauma can transcend into future generations by affecting the energy of genetics. If we learn to respond to negative circumstances with fear this too will be taught to children until they discover and implement healing. With this in mind it is worth questioning what the original trauma is that has been passed down to each generation. Could these variations of trauma just be derivatives of the original illusion of separation? Trauma is a mental process of reliving a past event as if it were happening in the present so while the event may be isolated in the past it is occurring right here and right now. We are currently living out the idea of separation as if it were true for us right now despite the mistake being made over two millennia ago.

Perhaps the way to bring about lasting change is to recognise the original source of pain that continues to reappear in the present moment. When we finally understand what the sponsoring thought is we realise we have been asking the wrong questions. There are no answers to meaningless questions that bear no relevance to truth, which is why our minds go into a frazzled attempt to provide solutions to problems it has made up. Such questions sound like; what did I do to deserve this? How can I repent for my wrongdoings? How did our world get to the state it is in now? Why we were banished to a life of hell? If we are all interconnected why do we live life as separate from source? There are no answers to these questions because they do not exist. The questions mask an implication that we are separate and therefore can only be asked if the person believes this is true. We do not need to continually live the physical manifestation of a thought that occurred many years ago for the trauma of separation never actually occurred. How can we be separate from that which we are? It is as spiritual teacher Mooji says, 'I don't have to be anything at all. I don't even have to be myself, because there is no such thing as not being myself. I am inescapably myself.'

Contemplate these affirmations:

I am not the mind that thinks, I am the presence that observes. I am the inner being that dwells in the heart completely supported by love, peace and joy. There is no need to do or be anything other than I am. My natural state of being is joy, wellness, ease and flow. I allow in the presence of my inner being by shedding a light unto the dark so that I may be free of lies that influence my experience. I intend to bridge the gap between thinking and my inner being so that I may live the physical manifestation of the oneness I truly am. There is no need for struggle or sacrifice on this planet for that insinuates a need for repentance. Separation is an illusion and I choose right now to return to my natural state of oneness. I choose to forgive myself for living a lie and others for teaching me the lie and I move into communion with my inner being. I am grateful for the light that always guides me home and today I choose to walk in its direction so that I may finally relinquish the illusion of separation and walk into the arms of love. I now see peace instead of pain.

3.6 Finding purpose in purposelessness

'Civilisation only produces in human beings a great variety of sensations and… decidedly nothing else.'

- Fyodor Dostoyevsky

Exchanging our worldview from one of attachment to freedom will help us reassess what is important and how best we can enjoy the pleasures life has to offer. As we have discovered, we have everything we need right now to be happy which means the external world holds no value that is essential to us. There is nothing that is needed by our inner being for it has everything. Material possessions, worldly success, relationships and money can flatter the fear mind and improve our quality of life but understanding that these things pose no benefit for the inner being relinquishes the desperate need for excessive acquisition of goods. That is not to say that we cannot enjoy or desire them but if we can shift our priority from the accumulation of wealth to connecting with our inner being through service we can enjoy the delights of the world with a refreshing lightness, which relieves the need for greed, frugality, neediness and possessiveness. We cannot take anything with us to heaven so why despair, fret, fight over, or latch onto anything that ultimately serves us in no way?

With this understanding there will be no extreme grief when material possessions suddenly disappear for we will know that life is ever changing and ever abundant. In this state, negative experiences will be seen as an invitation to change and will not escalate into trauma. Service does not necessarily imply giving up all material possessions and devoting all our spare time to planting trees, it means being of service to our true authentic self and clearing the channel for love. The greatest feeling comes from knowing we are living our purpose and by doing so fulfilling our wishes and enhancing the lives of others. When we are our true self others will feel inspired to wake up from their illusory slumber and walk towards the light of truth. That is true service.

The more we esteem the things we want the more important they become and block access to true awareness. When we no longer feel connection to our inner being we become addicted to external sources that fulfil our neediness. Until we realise that our needs are already met we will continue to look outside to the fill the void of emptiness as we cannot find worth in the worthless. Mental shifts naturally occur when we shed light on our apprehension and consistently refocus our awareness on the true self. Obsession is just like an addiction in that we use an external source to fill an emotional need. This can include obsessive worrying or stress and is generally considered unpleasant or unable to be helped.

We can find a way to release the need for destructive habits by internally fulfilling the need that causes us to look outside ourselves. Once we have identified the emotion behind the compulsion, which can usually be traced back to abandonment and lack of self love, we can incorporate habits that rewire the brain so that it consistently fills our internal longing for love. An effective way to begin the process of returning to the self is through affirmations as they are a form of intention. To some the idea of connecting with source may seem uninteresting, but boredom is simply a disguise for fear, which asks, 'who are we without our addictions? Who are we without neediness, illness, obsession or addiction?' Once the dream we have envisioned for our new life picks up momentum and grows bigger in our mind we will be pulled in with excitement and guided by anticipation rather than pushed by pain.

When we reactivate negative thoughts by talking about past events we simply activate a habit we think we need but if we choose to confront the fear, embrace it with our love and choose new thoughts the process of healing is vastly accelerated. Choose to end the suffering now by focusing awareness within. The more we disperse our energy outwardly the more vulnerable we are to the opinions and judgments of others, causing us to believe the fears of the world but when we show up as our true self we are at our greatest. When in doubt choose love. Inner transformation occurs when we can love who we once were and await with excitement for all the good that is speeding our way now. Let us no longer live life blind to our potential and a slave to obsessive negative thinking but instead awaken to the grace of our inner being and move in the direction of love. A feeling is just a thought and a thought can be changed. Eventually when we consistently direct our thoughts in the direction of love momentum will do the work for us and reciprocate with physical evidence. Helpful affirmations we can use on our journey of inner transformation include:

- I release the need to relive my past. I stand in the pure deliciousness of the present moment in anticipation for all the good that is speeding my way
- I choose now to embody the greatness I am meant to live
- I choose now to release the need to reactivate my past and enjoy all that I have in this moment
- Life is fun and exciting and I look forward to new and refreshing thoughts coming my way
- My past is no longer relevant to me and I embrace the new and exciting experiences coming my way
- Thinking new thoughts is fun and easy
- I have the power that creates worlds in my reach and I use it to transform my inner and outer world
- Relying on my inner world for encouragement will always uplift me

The experience can be enhanced during contemplative walks in nature or by listening to empowering music. Another tool that can be used to accelerate the process is to turn one affirmation into a narrative. For example we could say, 'I am so excited for what is about to come. I can feel myself standing on the brink of radical transformation and am beginning to see evidence of change in the way I feel and in the outside world. I love knowing that I am supported by life and I have the ability to choose whatever thought I think. I release the need to constantly relive my past and realise I cannot find myself in memories. I am so happy and grateful now that I am living my dream life and everyday is filled with exponential joy, love and peace. I am fulfilled by my work and love the people I choose to spend time with. New and exciting opportunities are on their way to me now.'

Repetition of the narrative strengthens its presence so that we begin to believe it and see physical evidence. We will most likely fall back into old habits along the way but with consistency and passion for our new vision we are able to persist and love the process. It takes more muscles for our face to form a frown than it does a smile and the same is true of negative thoughts. Depression and anxiety are draining emotions because they entail struggle and resistance to our natural state of being, but running from the pain also prolongs suffering as we will not hear the message it is attempting to communicate. When we listen to the message emerging through the pain we will more easily implement positive habits and uncover the refreshing lightness of being. Being our self requires no effort at all. Joy and love emerge when we are in communion with our truth.

3.7 Understanding the nature of fear

'Fear has made everything you think you see. All separation, all distinctions, and the multitude of difference you believe make up the world. They are not there. Love's enemy has made them up. Yet love can have no enemy, and so they have no cause, no being and no consequence. They can be valued, but remain unreal. They can be sought, but they cannot be found. Today we will not seek for them, nor waste this day in seeking what cannot be found.'

- A Course in Miracles

Fear can appear in many forms and in many varying degrees. Fear emerges from identification with the mind, which constantly faces near death experiences. As the mind lives in fear of meeting its death certain symptoms can arise spanning from panic attacks and intense dread to a vague sense of uneasiness. Eventually it can manifest into mental disorders and physical ailments as a psychological reaction to anything that deeply threatens its identity. The mind goes to much effort building a narrative out of all that happens in life and in doing so creates an identity that explains and validates its existence.

Narratives give the mind meaning and a purpose for existence that it literally cannot live without. Its purpose is to constantly anticipate future events that could threaten its existence, which usually leads to obsessive worrying, anticipation, dread and panic. Some people are able to manage the fear and continue daily life with only a slight hum in the back of their minds while others are unable to perform many basic tasks like leaving the house or catching public transport. The more power fear holds over us the more we want to turn away from it, but contrary to our instinctual reaction, when we turn towards the fear it loses power.

Our natural state of being allows and invites change but fear craves permanence and stability until eventually we live in fear of fear. Much anxiety is aroused in anticipation of anxiety, usually at a time and place that is inconvenient and involves judgment of other people. It is often described as a feeling of sheer terror, which is simply the mind expressing its fear of death. Our intention in the process of healing is not to kill anything but to shed light unto the darkness by facing the truth of what fear represents. When fear strikes there is usually a desire to seek refuge in an external manifestation of safety such as a home, job, or person. The mind is desperately trying to take on the role of God due to its belief that it has been abandoned and burdened with the responsibility of survival, a noble yet unnecessary feat that inspires feelings of hyper vigilance and scarcity.

Fear is a by-product of separation from source. In truth separation is impossible but when the mind believes the illusion it becomes a reality and acts in accordance with the illusion, which is then projected onto the outside world. We think fear thoughts and experience events that inspire more fear and when we conspire with others who are a vibrational match to fear the belief intensifies and is experienced as a catastrophe. The person who is in alignment with their true nature and in the presence of others who are not avoids being deeply affected by the catastrophe as their vision for love and joy outweighs the presence of fear and dismay. Fear holds no power when we fulfil its need for survival by acknowledging that we are in divine communion with spirit and forever protected by its grace. There is no need to act as God, there is no need to struggle and there is no need to seek for love and safety outside. We have everything we need in this moment right now to experience exponential joy, love and connection. Source is calling us to awaken to our true nature so we can relieve our mind of the burden to survive and enjoy what it means to live. Whether the fear we experience is intense or mild it is not too late now to relinquish our mind and surrender to the peace within.

When we open ourselves to the truth of our being our actions are executed out of a desire to create not to react. We no longer need to hustle and do things for the sake of preserving our reputation, instead we feel inspired to do things because it makes us feel good. When we are living our truth every task is done with passion and purpose for it is not the job title that reflects our purpose but the quality of engagement we give to the role. The more we practice coming into alignment with our inner being the more we will understand that what we see is not always what it seems and that most people react out of fear. It is often the people who insist on asserting their dominance that are the weakest, for the survival of their identity relies on the opinions of others whereas those who live their true nature do not need to be right for they have prioritised love not triumph.

The majority of the population has been taught to live in fear. When we understand this and take nothing they say personally we can relieve ourselves of the responsibility for other people's emotions. Only those who are hurting inside wish to hurt others and if we feel we have been hurt it is an indication of our own fear. Fear based relationships place limitations, conditions and expectations on others to provide the mind with a false sense of permanence. It wants to own others, establish an upper hand, and exert power through dominance or even submission yet this only brings about conflict, infidelity, disloyalty and heartache. The more we invest our identity in another person the more fragmented our energy becomes, and if the person begins to show signs of change or expansion our mind retaliates by constricting their freedom in the form of abuse, guilt tripping, gas lighting or blame.

The person whose identity is invested in another person requires permanence in the vibrational offering of the partner. They look for ways they can benefit from the relationship whether through status, power, emotional stability, reputation or sex. The person who recognises that fear seeks permanence and dominance understands that quality is brought to a relationship when we allow the person freedom to grow and change. Life's natural state of being is transience and people can either grow together or grow apart but what matters to the soul is not the growth of another but the growth of the self. Through the foggy goggles of fear we see all that we are not and when we remove them we will experience clarity and joy like no other. Happiness comes first and the rest thereafter is a compliment, not the other way around.

3.8 Choosing gratitude

'Each of us contains our ancestors and all the generations to come. When we free ourselves, we are freeing all humanity.'

- Paulo Coelho

Gratitude can often be depicted as a chore that requires one overlooking the frustration that comes from comparing their state of affairs to someone who supposedly has it better. It goes like, 'even though I detest most of my life and resent my neighbour who has it so much better, I am at least indebted to God for his decision for not banishing me to a life of poverty or third world living. Even though I experience depression and anxiety there are so many who have it worse than I do and I am grateful that I at least have the comfort of a functioning toilet.' This in fact expresses no thanks at all because it implies superiority over those who have less to be grateful for and entitlement when others have it better. It assumes that the only thing we have to be grateful for is wealth, health care and the suffering of others as a benchmark for our own happiness.

As a child you might have heard your parents say, 'I don't care if you're full, eat what's on your plate and be grateful you are not a starving child in Africa.' As adults we have been taught to use others suffering as a benchmark for gratitude. Who in their right mind would be grateful for suffering less while others suffer more? This frame of mind reactivates fear mindset so that we experience more poverty, depravation and competition. It implies that the only way to ensure happiness is for there to be another whose suffering is greater than ours. Similarly, when we express gratitude only when a desire manifests we create our life from the standpoint of lack as it implies that what we have now is not enough and we do not possess all we need to be happy in this moment. It also suggests that those who have more cause to be happy are to be envied and be brought down to our level. This is the fear mindset that once again provides evidence of the underlying assumption that we were abandoned at birth and separated from source. We may believe that in giving thanks at the expense of others is offering a vibration of wealth but in reality we are seeing with fear and will receive back experiences that reflect more lack.

So what exactly do we have to be grateful for? A better way we can phrase this question is what do we not have to be grateful for? Once we recognise that we have been given all that we need to live a life of greatness our vision of fear is replaced with love and in love there is enough for all. There is no one who is less entitled or less able to experience joy than another, which immediately abolishes the illusion of superiority and awakens us to the potential life has to offer. We have the same potential as the highest performing CEO's, the most revered pop stars and the most inspiring scientists. There is nothing that separates us from accessing the same potential for we are all connected to the same stream of wellbeing that offers all ideas. In the eyes of grace there are no victims, only choices and when we make the decision to live a life of greatness a shift in momentum occurs and we experience the magnificent flow of life. Life's love for us is so strong it places no limitations, restrictions or preferences on how we choose to live. We possess so much freedom that we are free to think we are trapped, a victim, or helpless if that is what we choose and life will support our vision by reflecting back to us evidence of those thoughts. As much as some crave to blame a higher entity for the state of their affairs, there is no one telling us what we can and cannot think, though life is aware of our suffering and is always guiding us home.

In the beginning it may feel like we are expressing appreciation in spite of what is going on but with enough consistency we will soon understand there is beauty in every experience. While negative circumstances may cause us to feel like a victim, love will give us clarity and we will see that everything is here to benefit our growth. There are no accidents, no punishment and no praise for what we do on earth because the point of existence is to fully experience the potential of who we are. Attention flows energy towards what we are focused on and increases the weight of momentum so when we are appreciating something we are creating a point of attraction that compliments good feelings. Feeling good about what we are focusing on compounds energy by bringing to us experiences that will elicit more of those good feeling emotions. When the experience shows up enough times the process of manifestation becomes effortless.

When we are attached to an outcome and expect a particular experience we are creating from a place of lack as we do not believe in the timeless love and support the universe has for us. Releasing dogmatic attachment to conditions, freeing ourselves and others of limitations and living in a state of appreciation for the unconditional love life has for us will attract a life of love. Learning to continuously flow our attention to what we appreciate will help us see life with rose coloured glasses. This might look like appreciating the warmth of the sun, the vibrant colours of the leaves, the wonderful people who support us, our own tenacity, our willingness to be open minded, the bed we sleep on, the delicious food that nourishes our body or our body's unconditional love for us. The more we practice this the more we realise that there is much to be grateful for and when we are in the state of appreciation we create circumstance that gives us more to appreciate.

3.9 When the fear mind attacks

'Luck is what happens when preparation meets opportunity.'

- Seneca

The fear mind can find nothing to be grateful for as it always living in expectation of unmet desires. Nothing is ever enough and yet it believes it deserves everything. When others achieve success the fear mind finds a way to justify it with excuses like, 'why can't that happen for me,' or 'I bet they didn't even work as hard as I have.' It is jealous, it seeks ways to bring others down to their level, it justifies why they are the way they are and is stubborn in its thinking. The fear mind attacks others and finds things to complain about to elicit sympathy from others and reaffirm its decision to stay stuck in its ways. It rejects self-growth and shuts down when someone attempts to counter its point of view with a more enlightening way of being.

The fear mind is also evident in people who belittle others as a way of enforcing their dominance but this is only defending their belief that they themselves are inferior and must bring others down with them. One thing to keep in mind with bullies is that people only bring others down when the other person has something they want, whether it be good looks, health, wealth, loving relationships or self-confidence. They may either want to take the desired attribute for themselves or strip the other person of it so that they are empty also. Mistreatment can also be disguised as productivity especially when a manager abuses his staff for the purpose of increasing production. Often our instinct is to complain about the person behind their back, avoid them, agree with them to avoid conflict or dispute their behaviour but all of these involve assuming we are at the mercy of the difficult person, or in other words, a victim. So what is the appropriate way of handling the situation?

Understand that the fear mind will want to attack the person that threatens our sense of identity but the mind that dwells in the heart of truth realises that if the actions of the person bother us they are simply reflecting back the illusion that blocks our path to peace. If we are clear in our vibrational offering their actions will bypass our experience or not bother us. Finding fault in the other person bypasses the truth that we are seeing something that is not there, so while we may think the other person is to blame for our unhappiness they are reflecting back to us a quality we also possess. The fear mind seeks to find ways to keep the self small and will happily accept the identity of a victim because that proves suffering is real, but what it is refuses to accept is that our emotions are not caused externally, they are chosen by us. Remember that the world is our thoughts made manifest so if a person is bothering us, what are they showing? Once the real cause of the upset has been identified our judgment of the person goes from a bully to a teacher and we can express gratitude to the universe for providing us with the tools to reveal the cause of suffering. The energy of the situation will naturally shift and change in a way that pleases us either by seeing the person replaced, seeing their behaviour changed, being unaffected by their actions or all of them combined. Once the lesson is learned the universe will dissolve the situation with ease.

The fear mind identifies as a seeker because it constantly looks outside the self for ways to validate its existence and prolong its suffering but never finds anything to satisfy its needs because it does not exist. The mind is aware that it will never find anything but will persist in cementing its identity as a victim through the act of seeking. It will say, 'see? Life is a constant disappointment and cannot provide me all that I need to be happy. God has abandoned me and I must suffer to have my desires met.' What a depressing way to see life! The only way to end the illusion of suffering is to recognise the illusion for what it is and rectify our thinking with the love that is bursting inside us. There is nothing life has not provided us with to compliment our experience on earth and it all begins when we question if looking outside ourselves will truly bring satisfaction. Once we recognise that life loves us unconditionally and is always guiding us home our perception of life will truly change and anything we previously saw as difficult will become a great teacher. All paths lead to one destination; home. The only duty we have in life is to align with the stream of wellbeing that flows to and through us and become a physical demonstration to others that a life without suffering is entirely possible. True service is embodying all that we are so others too may be guided to their own truth. Everything we witness today is a product of a past thought but we have the choice in the present moment to choose a different thought. That is deliberate creation.

Considering the reality of this new way of creation requires a certain degree of open mindedness and a willingness to replace fear with love by recognising that we are not the product of our thoughts. Our reality is simply a manifestation of our thoughts and our thoughts are meaningless for they are nothing but an opinion about a past experience. True presence requires no thought. As you read you will most likely recognise ways you have been holding yourself apart from truth and that you are not totally innocent in conflict even if it appears you are the victim to the actions of another. Understand that the majority of the world's population have been taught to live in fear and will continue to teach their young the same habits of thought for that is the way they know how to 'survive' their perceived reality.

In truth there are no mistakes or accidents, only choices and for much of our lives we have chosen to live in ignorance of the truth. Understand that we made the choice to live another's lies and that we can choose to change right now. There is no need to blame another or ourselves for what our choice of thoughts has manifested for until we are shown that struggle is unnecessary we believe we are doing our best. Guilt, shame and punishment are thoughts of the fear mind but know that we can do no wrong and it is never too late to awaken to the truth. Forgiveness is also an attribute of fear because it assumes that wrong can be done but if we see with the eyes of love we will know that we are all doing our best to find our way home so have patience with your learning and force no one else to follow you. Everyone has the freedom to choose love or suffering and when they are ready they will choose to change so let us take our attention off the progress of others and focus on our own growth. Once we are in connection with our stream of wellbeing we will experience an inner peace and joy that becomes so infectious people will not be able to help but ask how they can have some of what we have got.

3.10 Influencing change in others

'Ego is no more than this: identification with form, which primarily means thought forms. If evil has any reality – and it has a relative, not an absolute, reality – this is also its definition: complete identification with form – physical forms, thought forms, emotional forms. This results in a total unawareness of my connectedness with the whole, my intrinsic oneness with every 'other' as well as with the Source. This forgetfulness is original sin, suffering, delusion.'

- Eckhart Tolle

During our journey of inner transformation a shift in consciousness will occur. This shift will awaken in us the truth we have always known and inspires us to make the changes needed to invite peace in our life. It will arouse in us a persistence and dedication to create a life of greatness that goes far beyond the acquisition of material possessions for soon nothing in the outside world will satisfy. We will not identify with the world of our thoughts but will instead use them as a tool for creating the world of our dreams both internally and externally. When we awaken to our truth and replace our judgment with love we can use our thoughts to create a consistent state of joy, love and peace so that we do not succumb to old habitual thoughts of limitation and judgment. We are a clear channel for the source of all ideas, inspiration and creativity to flow through so we will receive assistance clearly and quickly. To others we will look like a powerhouse of creativity and focus but to us it will feel like the most natural state of being. No longer will we suffer the perceived 'mistreatment' of life's quarrels and react out of fear and victimhood because we will have grown too big to ever feel comfortable being that small again. We will remain an ordinary human being but what emerges will be magnificent. We will feel the incredible lightness of being and treat every experience as a blessing.

When we place importance on the creations of the fear mind they expand in our minds and prolong its affects but when we realise they are a mere illusion we can choose again. It is as Thomas Jefferson said, 'If you want something you've never had, you have to do something you've never done.' If we want to see change in our life we must be willing to change from within, otherwise nothing will change at all. We must be willing to become aware of the fear mind's rapacious need to acquire things for the fulfilment of its identity and separate ourselves from those thoughts that dictate habits and actions. Ask, 'Who am I really?' If we are the one observing and experiencing our circumstances then how can we exist in them? We cannot be what we see, we can only trick ourselves into thinking we are it and the moment we break association our true self emerges and we will begin to merge with oneness. We give up the illusion of separation or rather the illusion that there is something to be given up. Once this is done our priority will shift from greed and neediness to connection with our inner being. We will be naturally inspired to change our habits so that they bring about the change we wish to see, which might show up as gratuitous thoughts, healthy eating, helping others, self care, improved job performance, pursuit of interests or all of them combined. No matter what accumulates in wealth, the cost of pain, suffering, anxiety, guilt, fear, and shame cannot tempt the one that stands in the pure deliciousness of truth.

Those who emulate the essence of truth in their way of being emanate a sense of peace that is contagious and felt by all, including the fear mind in others. Some may feel inspired to replicate our journey of inner peace and others may wish to fight it by questioning the validity of our truth. Those that feel inspired are ready to be lead home and those that attack are so encumbered by fear they suppress the desire for freedom by attacking what threatens the safety of entrapment. Pay attention if you are one of these people who use excuses to avoid coming into alignment with your inner being. You may be fooled into thinking it is safer to stay small but what the mind fears most is the death of itself, yet know that when the dark is shone upon by the light what dies is the illusion of separation. This is the greatest threat to the small self and so the mind will try to disguise its point of view as spiritual or enlightened but don't let it fool you. Fear may be clever but it is not intelligent. Know that in the relinquishment of fear we are giving up nothing, as there was nothing to begin with. Fear is empty, a state of mind, and an idea that is born out of separation and when we reconnect with source freedom emerges. Therefore let us treat our current way of thinking as an illness. Once we recognise that the thoughts we think are an ailment we can take the action needed to get us in our right mind. To rediscover our true nature we need to lose our minds and find a cure for the epidemic of negative thinking that is the cause of virtually all ailments and crisis.

As we progress on this journey of awareness we will more easily identify symptoms of negative thinking in others and ourselves. Let us not succumb to the media's attempt to arouse fear for nothing has gone wrong. In fact, recognition of adversity is the first step in initiating a revolution as we have discovered and will soon gain momentum by attracting people who actively participate in the evolution of our thinking. Assist those who are willing to be shown another way and present to the fear mind a new way of being but do not judge or intercept the learning of others for that deprives them the joy of finding their own way home. With gentle persistence and presentation of new thoughts we can encourage others to look within without the need to convince them of their wrongdoings and dogmatically insist upon them our idea that we are right. Remember fear requires superiority and love requires nothing, not even the need to be heard or recognised for it dwells in pure awareness. Trust not those who dogmatically enforce their ideas for that is evidence of fear. True love does not need to convince others of its truth, it simply embodies it and guides those who are willing to listen. Love does not judge, interfere, argue or protest; it listens, guides, remembers and exercises patience. When we are strong in the vibration we are offering it does not matter whether someone agrees or disagrees with us, we are pure in our thoughts and require nothing from anybody. That is true freedom. That is love.

3.11 Coming home

'To live is the rarest thing in the world. Most people exist, that is all.'
- Oscar Wilde

There are no 'how to' books, strategies or tools that could ever teach us that which has no words. The journey of inner transformation is a personal quest that can only attract guidance and arouse an inner knowingness. This knowingness informs all of our decisions and dictates how much joy we allow into our lives. The more we deepen our connection to the self the richer our experience becomes. Love is not something that can be achieved, it is an undeniable state of being that is forever present and can only appear as absent under the blanket of illusion. When we awaken to this illusion it is impossible to turn our head away from the infinite potential that is at our fingertips.

Fear is a cheap, synthetic reaction to life born from the idea that we exist to suffer, not to thrive. Many people allow their thinking to be ruled by fear and limit what they allow themselves to experience. Rather than seeing themselves as creators they live out the reality of victimhood and try to find themselves in the outside world that is in actuality nothing but a reflection of collective thought. Fear can exist only in the mind and the more we use our mind to understand our purpose in life the more fear we will encounter. In order to lose our mind and unlock the potential for greatness we must be prepared to venture into the unknown for a short while as our identity shifts from fear to oneness. Only when this is achieved can we experience the exponential love life has to offer. Ignoring the call to greatness will prolong feelings of stagnation and limitation.

The call to return home is a personal choice everyone has the freedom to make at any time they choose. It is neither a requirement nor a responsibility; it is an invitation. Love requires nothing it only gives. When we accept the invitation we become a medium for great ideas and a channel for greatness to enrich the world around us without any effort. Love becomes the driving force when we become a recipient to the potential for peace. Extreme negative emotions will no longer plague our state of being and we will be able to dissociate with external circumstances causing pain. We will have developed the skills to transform adversity into opportunity and infuse love into any situation.

An incredible light shines in the eyes of those who have chosen to accept the invitation to return home for they live in the awareness that all is well. These people are free of resentment, free of trauma, and free of attachment. Love is the only thing on their mind and the only thing they strive for. They are naturally at the service of others as a living demonstration of what is possible when we live life in the hands of spirit. They have treated the illness of negative thought and in doing so bloomed from identification as the small, fearful, traumatised person to the beautiful, inspired, fully fledged being of love. This person dreams big, demands greatness and allows nothing to compromise their state of joy. They live in the afterlife. This person is you.

About The Author

Author Kirsty Stewart was born in Sydney, Australia and educated at the University of Canberra. Driven by a personal quest to deepen her understanding of suffering Kirsty was drawn to the philosophical inquiries of some of the greatest spiritual teachers. Passionate about the wellbeing of the planet she teaches how to move towards a vision of greatness by transforming the inner world from one of pain to love.

You're Doing Great Sweetie

9 781647 861094